First published 2004
Published by Ken Kostick in arrangement with Sunbeam Corporation (Canada) Limited

Copyright ® Ken Kostick, 2004

All rights reserved. No part of this book may be used or reproduced in any manner
whatsoever without written permission of the Publisher.
Printed in Canada by Advertek Printing

Kostick, Ken
Countertop to Table Cuisine
ISBN 0-9735249-0-1

Creative development and design by Urban advertising + design, Hamilton, ON
Original photography by Banko Photographic Ltd., Hamilton, ON
Art direction by Trevor Shaw
Food styling by James Scott
Hair and makeup by Melissa Diluliis

Oster® kitchen appliances supplied by Sunbeam Corporation (Canada) Limited

The Publisher and Sunbeam Corporation (Canada) Limited expressly disclaim any
responsibility for any liability, loss, or risk, personal or otherwise, which is incurred
as a consequence, directly or indirectly, of the use and application of any of the
contents of this book.

To my wonderful parents,
Ed and Helen Kostick,
who encouraged me to pursue my dreams
and taught me very early the joy of food, family and sharing with others.

Love You Always!
Ken

Countertop to Table Cuisine

by KEN KOSTICK

Enjoy exciting, satisfying, hearty and healthy meals using the latest kitchen appliance technology from the Oster® division. All of the recipes are easy, convenient and, best of all; they're healthy because you make them yourself from fresh ingredients you can buy at any grocery store.

- Unforgettable hors d'oeuvres
- Healthy snacks
- High-energy morning shakes
- Quick and satisfying lunches
- Hearty soups and stews
- Delicious main courses
- Decadent desserts

Quality cuisine like you'd find in fine restaurants all made in your kitchen, from your fresh ingredients – without ever turning on your stove. This is the "how-to-book" that will have you using your convenient countertop kitchen appliances every day to help create a healthy lifestyle for you and your entire family.

contents

The most fun I've ever had writing recipes!

I have to tell you that putting together this book has been the most fun I have ever had creating recipes. My goal when I set out was to never turn on the stove and to use the countertop appliances that can be found in almost everyone's kitchen. As I tried new recipes and became more familiar with each appliance I realized that the uses for today's countertop appliances are limitless. Take the time, as I did, to familiarize yourself with all the features on the units and experiment on your own – the results are worth it.

I want to thank the Oster® division for the inspiration and for supplying the appliances to make this book possible. I have truly enjoyed the opportunity to show you how to make delicious, healthy meals every day from fresh ingredients, in minimal time, all using these wonderful convenient products. And speaking of time, when entertaining at home, using these appliances creatively can not only help you serve your guests the very best, but also allow you to spend more time with your guests and not in the kitchen.

Here's to convenience…delicious food…and having more fun cooking creatively.

Ken Kostick

Ken Kostick on health, nutrition and the joy of preparing and eating delicious homemade meals every day of the week.

Why don't we eat healthy?

For most of us, the answer is simple. We're very busy with jobs, kids, housekeeping, hobbies, family obligations and maintaining some sort of social life. Preparing dinner has taken on a new dimension – take-out. Take out from the restaurant or take out something from the freezer. Sure it's quick, always convenient and sometimes necessary. But we know that it's not a healthy alternative to good homemade, balanced meals.

We all know how to improve our health. Eat lots of fresh fruits and vegetables every day. Eat lean red meat, fowl or fish in moderation. Eat whole grain breads and cereals that are high in fiber and low in sugar. Drink fruit juices without added sugar and drink plenty of water throughout the day. And try to get at least thirty minutes of exercise every day. We know that's what will keep us healthy, fight off disease and give us the energy and mental edge we need to get through our day.

So what do most of us do? We call coffee with cream and sugar breakfast, pop a frozen waffle in the toaster for the kids and pick up a high fat doughnut or muffin on the way to work. If we go out for lunch, it's usually the closest fast food outlet. Then we navigate the rush hour traffic and pick up dinner on the way home. After helping kids with homework, doing a load of laundry or sorting through some bills, we fall exhausted onto the couch and wonder why we don't have more energy.

I believe you can live a healthier life.
That's why I've written this book.

You can shop for fresh nutritious foods. You can prepare a delicious, satisfying meal for you and your family every night of the week. How? Simply by utilizing your countertop kitchen appliances that you don't realize are so versatile. If you don't have the appliances used in these recipes, read them over, see how easy they are and you'll realize that investing in these appliances will save you a lot of preparation time and put you on a healthier road.

Grocery stores are responding to their customers' desire to eat healthier. Many stores today have in-store bakeries with breads, rolls and desserts made fresh – without preservatives. Butchers in the meat department will trim the fat from your favourite cut of meat. There is fresh fish and seafood available thanks to modern shipping methods that bring the catch from the ocean to the store in just a few hours. Best of all, visit the fresh fruits and vegetables section, and think seriously about paying that little bit extra for organically grown produce. Not only is it healthier, it tastes fresher, crisper and more flavourful. We are so lucky to have all this available to us. With just a bit of time and effort we can cut down on the unwanted preservatives, excess fats, salt and sugar found in prepared foods and eat happier and healthier.

In creating the recipes for this book, each one had to meet three simple, but specific criteria. As you read through these wonderful recipes and see how they can all be prepared in just a few easy steps, I think you'll agree that I've achieved my goal.

1. They had to be healthy, nutritious and gourmet delicious – the kind of appetizers, salads, soups, entrées and desserts you'd find in the finest restaurants.

2. They had to be easy, quick and convenient to prepare using fresh ingredients you can find in any grocery store.

3. They had to be completely prepared using convenient, energy and time saving countertop appliances.

I believe that there is nothing more important than good health; and if you want to know exactly what is in the food you eat you must prepare your meals yourself.

I believe that taking the time to prepare a delicious, healthy meal for yourself and those you care about is a creative, expressive, and emotionally satisfying endeavor.

Most of all, I believe that cooking should be fun. Some of my most precious childhood memories are of mornings spent in the kitchen with my father trying new recipes and working together to create delicious, hearty meals we would enjoy together. Cooking is family, friends, and fun – cooking is life.

I want to thank the Oster® division for letting me use their wonderful products and for making this book possible. I want to thank the people who worked with me – the designers, photographers and editors, as well as my friends and fellow chefs who helped me test and refine these recipes. Finally, I want to thank you for buying this book and believing, as I do, that we can live happier, healthier lives simply by taking a few extra minutes each day to create delicious meals that everyone will enjoy.

I hope you try each and every one of these recipes and I truly hope my book makes a difference in your life.

Ken Kostick
Toronto, Canada
October 2004

About This Book

What ends up as dinner often depends on how much time you have to cook and what's in the fridge. So this book is organized to make finding the right recipe just as quick and easy as preparing the meals themselves. The book is divided into colour-coded sections with each section containing recipes that were created using the featured appliance for that section. So meals prepared primarily with the rice cooker will be in Rice Cooker section distinguished by the color band down the edge of the page, although quite often more than one Oster® appliance is used in the preparation of a recipe. Check the Table of Contents for a complete listing of the sections and the recipes in that section.

As you read the recipes you'll notice that there are "variations" and "tips" that can help you prepare the dish in different ways to accommodate individual preferences. You'll find tips on replacing the main ingredient, e.g., chicken for pork or fish for seafood, to give you a greater variety of dishes. You'll also find tips for using lower fat ingredients, vegetarian versions, spicy alternatives or how to serve the dish as an appetizer.

Finally, at the back you'll find a cross-referenced index that will quickly show you where you can find every recipe in the book. Look under "C" for chicken and you'll find a complete listing of all the chicken recipes, including the ones where chicken is suggested as a possible replacement. You'll also find the chicken recipes listed under specific categories, so Chicken Soup will be under the Soups listing and Chicken Salad will be under the Salads.

My suggestion is to leaf through the book and read the recipes. When you find one you think you'd like to try soon, either note it on the Table of Contents page or write the name and page number on a separate piece of paper and keep it with the book. Then when you're making your shopping list, you'll have quick access to the recipes and ingredients you'll need.

I'm hoping that this is one cookbook you'll use often to prepare fresh, wholesome meals that will make your life both easier and healthier. Enjoy!

For Ken Kostick and his healthy, active lifestyle – the world truly is his Oster®.

Every recipe in this book was created using these
Oster® products.

Oster® In2itive® Blender/Food Processor

Oster® 12-Speed Core Blender

Oster® Blend-N-Go® Cup

Oster® Inspire® Food Processor

Oster® 12-Cup Programmable Coffeemaker

Oster® Coffee Burr Mill

Oster® Digital Food Steamer

Oster® Inspire® Rice Cooker

Oster® Inspire® 6-Slice Toaster Oven

Oster® Commercial Style Deep Fryer

Oster® Inspire® Electric Skillet

Oster® Inspire® Indoor Grill

COUNTERTOP TO TABLE CUISINE

RICE COOKER

It's not just for rice!

This is no doubt the most under-utilized appliance in the kitchen. Just look at all the wonderful dishes you can make – soups, stews, chili, Jambalaya and much more. And you do it all so quickly and easily. Just put in the ingredients, push the button and you're free to do something else until the 'keep warm' light comes on and your meal is ready. And with the non-stick pot, clean up takes mere seconds. I hope you enjoy my recipes and once you see what this versatile appliance can do maybe you'll come up with a few of your own.

Red Wine Mushroom Risotto
South American-Style Beans & Rice with Coriander
Orange Rice with Shrimp & Cointreau
Lobster Seafood Stew with Fresh Lime & Tarragon
Chili, Chili & More Chili
Vegetarian Chili with Apple & Cinnamon
Rainbow Vegetable Rice with Fresh Basil
Apple Rice with Lamb & a Hint of Cinnamon
Smoked Salmon with Orange & Grand Marnier Soup
Mushroom Soup Galore
Lazy Jambalaya
Espresso Basil Beef Stew with Red Wine & Dijon

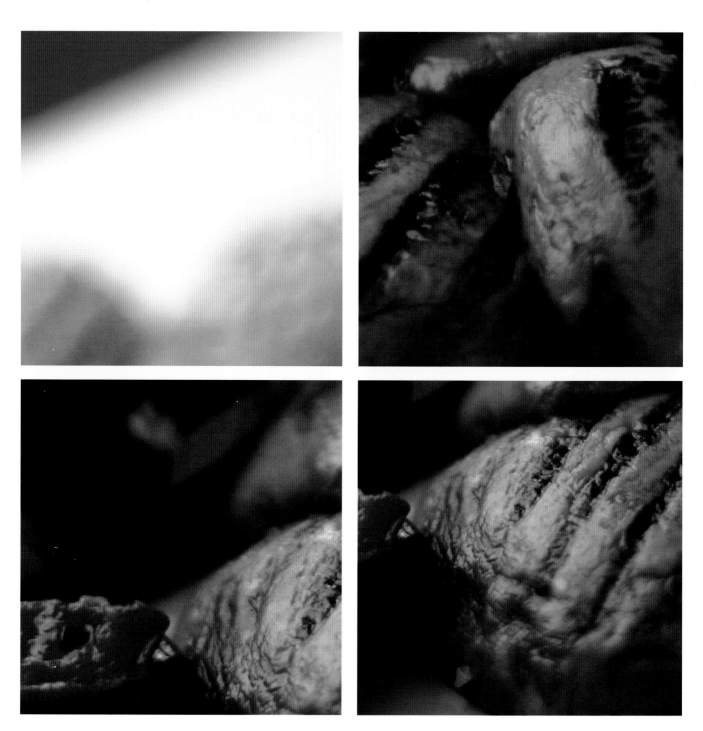

Red Wine Mushroom Risotto

INGREDIENTS

1 small sweet red pepper, seeded and coarsely chopped

3 cloves garlic OR 1 tsp (5 mL) bottled minced garlic

1 small red onion, coarsely chopped

20 to 25 medium-sized button mushrooms, coarsely chopped (approx. 3 cups/750 mL)

3 large portobello mushrooms, coarsely chopped

1/4 cup (50 mL) chopped fresh basil OR 1 tsp (5 mL) dried

3 tbsp (45 mL) olive oil

1 1/2 cups (325 mL) arborio rice

5 cups (1.25 L) vegetable stock OR chicken stock

1/2 cup (125 mL) dry red wine

1/2 tsp (2 mL) salt

1/2 tsp (2 mL) black pepper

1/2 cup (125 mL) whipping cream

1/2 cup (125 mL) freshly grated Parmesan cheese

SERVES 4 TO 6

METHOD

1. In a blender or food processor, combine red pepper, garlic, onion, mushrooms and basil. Set to pulse or chop until vegetables are finely chopped and well combined.

2. Transfer vegetable mixture to rice cooker and add oil, rice, stock, red wine, salt and pepper. Cover and cook until "warm" light illuminates, approximately 20 to 25 minutes.

3. Once done, add the whipping cream and Parmesan cheese and stir well until risotto has a creamy texture.

APPETIZER TIP
Use as a starter or appetizer on small salad plates

STEAMER OPTION
Coat 2 chicken breasts with olive oil and rosemary, salt and pepper. Steam while risotto is cooking.

Although this makes for a great entrée, I often serve this tasty dish on small plates, as a starter to the main meal.

CHANGE IT UP

VARIATION
Substitute 2 cups shrimp, scallops or fresh crabmeat for mushrooms

Substitute button, cremini or shiitake for portobello mushrooms

ADDITION
Coat 2 skinless, boneless chicken breasts with olive oil and rosemary, salt and pepper. Steam while risotto is cooking. Once cooked, slice chicken and serve on rice.

LOWER FAT OPTION
If you want a lower-fat risotto, leave out the whipping cream and substitute with a low-fat or non-fat soup stock

COUNTERTOP TO TABLE CUISINE

South American-Style Beans & Rice with Coriander

INGREDIENTS

3 cloves garlic OR 1 tsp (5 mL) bottled minced garlic

2 celery stalks, coarsely chopped

1 green pepper, seeded and coarsely chopped

1 sweet red pepper, seeded and coarsely chopped

1 medium red onion, peeled and coarsely chopped

2 tbsp (30 mL) olive oil

1 tsp (5 mL) chili powder

2 cups (500 mL) mild salsa

2 tbsp (30 mL) freshly squeezed lemon juice

$1/_2$ tsp (2 mL) dried basil

$1/_2$ tsp (2 mL) sea salt

$1/_2$ tsp (2 mL) black pepper

1 19-oz can (540 mL) red kidney beans, rinsed and drained

1 cup (250 mL) white rice

2 cups (500 mL) vegetable stock

$1/_2$ cup (125 mL) chopped fresh coriander

SERVES 4

METHOD

1. In a blender or food processor, combine garlic, celery, peppers, onion and coriander. Set to pulse or chop until vegetables are finely chopped and well mixed.

2. Transfer vegetable mixture to a rice cooker and add oil, chili powder, salsa, lemon juice, basil, salt, pepper, beans, rice, and stock. Cover and cook until "warm" light illuminates.

3. As soon as "warm" light is on, remove lid and add coriander. Stir, remove beans and rice from cooker, and serve.

It's the chili and salsa that give this dish its latin flavour, but it's the coriander, which is indigenous to southeast Asia, that makes it truly multi-cultural. This is hearty enough to serve as a one-dish meal, with toasted fajitas on the side.

CHANGE IT UP

VARIATION

If you don't have – or don't like – coriander, substitute with chopped fresh flat-leaf parsley (also known as Italian parsley)

ADDITION

Add 6 to 8 peeled and deveined raw jumbo shrimp or 2 boneless, skinless chicken breasts to rice cooker's steamer and steam as the rice and beans are cooking. Once rice is done, add cooked shrimp or chicken before serving.

SPICY

Add 1 jalapeno chili pepper, seeded and chopped, with the rest of the spices. Jalapenos are available fresh or canned. If using fresh, remember to wear rubber gloves when seeding and chopping.

Orange Rice with Shrimp & Cointreau

INGREDIENTS

1 small red onion, peeled and coarsely chopped

1 sweet red pepper, seeded and coarsely chopped

2 medium carrots, peeled and chopped

2 small seedless oranges, peeled and chopped

2 tbsp (30 mL) olive oil

1½ cups (375 mL) white rice

3 cups (750 mL) orange juice

1 tbsp (15 mL) grated orange zest

2 tbsp (30 mL) Cointreau liqueur

½ tsp (2 mL) dried tarragon

½ tsp (2 mL) sea salt

½ tsp (2 mL) black pepper

20 medium-large frozen cooked shrimp, peeled and deveined

SERVES 4 TO 6

METHOD

1. In a blender or food processor, combine onion, pepper, carrots and the oranges. Set to pulse or chop until ingredients are finely chopped and well combined.

2. Transfer the vegetable-orange mixture to a rice cooker and add oil, rice, orange juice, zest, tarragon, Cointreau, salt and pepper.

3. Cover and cook for about 10 minutes.

4. Add the shrimp and complete the cooking process. The meal will be complete when the "warm" light illuminates.

If you've never had orange-flavoured rice before, you're in for a real treat. The Cointreau in this rice dish underscores the orange-scented rice and the addition of shrimp will take you over the moon. If you don't eat seafood, you can substitute 2 cups chopped cooked chicken for shrimp, or even with 1 cup chopped tofu.

CHANGE IT UP

VARIATION

For more tropical fare, substitute the orange, orange zest and orange juice with 2 cups (500 mL) chopped pineapple and 3 cups (750 mL) pineapple juice. Add half cup (125 mL) shredded unsweetened coconut for added flavour.

ADDITION

Supplement the shrimps with 6 to 8 small, or medium, cooked scallops and half cup (125 mL) chopped cooked baby squid

Lobster Seafood Stew with Fresh Lime & Tarragon

INGREDIENTS

1 small red onion, peeled and coarsely chopped

2 cloves garlic, chopped OR 1/2 tsp (2 mL) bottled minced garlic

1 small fennel bulb, coarsely chopped

2 celery stalks, coarsely chopped

2 carrots, peeled and coarsely chopped

Juice of 3 limes

1 19-oz (540 mL) can diced stewed tomatoes, undrained

1/4 cup (50 mL) chopped fresh tarragon

6 cups (1.5 L) vegetable stock

1 tbsp (15 mL) granulated sugar

1/2 tsp (2 mL) sea salt

1 tsp (5 mL) black pepper

1 cooked lobster 1 to 2 lbs (450 to 900 g) in shell OR 2 cups cooked canned lobster

1 to 2 lbs (450 to 900 g) raw mussels in shell

1 cup (250 mL) canned clams, drained

2 cups (500 mL) medium-large raw shrimp, peeled and deveined

SERVES 4 TO 6

METHOD

1. In a blender or food processor, combine onion, garlic, fennel, celery and carrots. Set to pulse or chop until vegetables are finely chopped and well combined.

2. Transfer the vegetable mixture to rice cooker and add tarragon, lime juice, tomatoes, stock, sugar, salt and pepper. Cook for about 10 minutes.

3. Add the lobster (if whole, in the shell), mussels, clams and shrimp and continue cooking until the "warm" light illuminates, this will take approximately 12 to 15 minutes more.

4. Remove seafood stew and serve, discarding any mussel shells that have remained unopened after cooking.

This tasty stew is a perfect meal for a dinner party: it's well worth the effort. If using a live lobster, place in rice cooker at the start of cooking process, but if you don't have the inclination to boil a live lobster, you can get frozen lobster tails or canned cooked lobster.

CHANGE IT UP

VARIATION
Substitute scallops for shrimp and coriander, basil or flat-leaf parsley for tarragon

SPICY
Add 1 jalapeno chili pepper, seeded and chopped, to step 1

Chili, Chili, & More Chili

INGREDIENTS

1 lb (450 g) lean ground beef

1 small red onion, peeled and coarsely chopped

3 cloves garlic, chopped OR 1 tsp (5 mL) bottled minced garlic

1 small sweet red pepper, seeded and coarsely chopped

1 small green pepper, seeded and coarsely chopped

1 small jalapeno chili pepper, seeded and chopped (optional) OR 1 tsp (5 ml) hot sauce

3 celery stalks, coarsely chopped

1 28-oz (796 mL) can diced stewed tomatoes, undrained

$1/2$ cup (125 mL) dry red wine

1 19-oz (540 mL) can red kidney beans, rinsed and drained

$1/2$ cup (125 mL) unsweetened apple juice

2 tbsp (30 mL) chili powder

$1/2$ cup (125 mL) chopped flat-leaf parsley

$1/2$ tsp (2 mL) sea salt

1 tsp (5 mL) black pepper

CHANGE IT UP

LOWER FAT OPTION	ADDITION
Substitute the lean ground beef with lean ground turkey	Add 2 small cups espresso to add a way-down-south flavour to this down-home meal

SERVES 6 TO 8

METHOD

1. In a rice cooker set to "on", add the lean ground beef and stir with a spatula, sautéing about 10 minutes or until browned. Turn off rice cooker and set aside.

2. Meanwhile, in a blender or food processor, combine onion, garlic, peppers, jalapeno (if using) and celery. (You may have to do this in two separate batches.) Set to pulse or chop until vegetables are finely chopped and well combined.

3. Transfer vegetable mixture to rice cooker and add tomatoes, red wine, juice, kidney beans, chili powder, salt and pepper. Turn on the rice cooker and cook until the "warm" light illuminates, this should take approximately 18 to 20 minutes.

4. When cooked, remove lid and add parsley. Mix and serve.

VEGETARIAN OPTION
Replace the beef with $3/4$ cup (175 mL) textured vegetable protein, which can be found in most health food stores, or with 2 cups (500 mL) chopped firm tofu.

ENTERTAINING TIP
To make dip: Add I cup (250 mL) salsa to a chilled bowl of chili and top with a dollop of sour cream.

LEFTOVER TIP
To make an incredibly delicious pasta sauce, add 1 cup (250 mL) chili to 1 cup (250 mL) tomato sauce; place in a saucepan and heat on medium high, stirring, until sauce begins to bubble. Remove and pour over pasta.

Vegetarian Chili with Apple & Cinnamon

INGREDIENTS

1 small red onion, peeled and coarsely chopped

2 cloves garlic, chopped OR $1/2$ tsp (2 mL) bottled minced garlic

2 celery stalks, coarsely chopped

2 medium carrots, coarsely chopped

1 cup (250 mL) chopped button mushrooms

1 small green pepper, seeded and coarsely chopped

1 small sweet red pepper, seeded and coarsely chopped

2 apples, peeled, cored and chopped

1 28-oz (796 mL) can diced stewed tomatoes, undrained

1 19-oz (540 mL) can red kidney beans, rinsed and drained

$1/2$ cup (125 mL) textured vegetable protein (optional)

$1/2$ tsp (2 mL) dried basil OR 2 tbsp (15 mL) chopped fresh

1 cup (250 mL) vegetable stock OR unsweetened apple juice

1 tbsp (15 mL) granulated sugar

$1/2$ tsp (2 mL) ground cinnamon

$1/2$ tsp (2 mL) sea salt

$1/2$ tsp (2 mL) black pepper

SERVES 4 TO 6

METHOD

1. In a blender or food processor, combine onion, garlic, celery, carrots, mushrooms, peppers, and apples. Set to pulse or chop until vegetables are finely chopped and well combined. (You may have to do this in two batches.)

2. Transfer vegetable mixture to rice cooker and add tomatoes, beans, textured vegetable protein (if using), basil, stock, sugar, cinnamon, salt and pepper cook until "warm" light illuminates.

ENTERTAINING TIP
To make dip: In a bowl, combine 1 cup (250 ml) chili and 1 cup (250 mL) salsa and a dollop of sour cream

LEFTOVER TIP
To make pasta sauce: Combine 1 cup (250 mL) of chili and 1 cup (250 mL) of tomato sauce; place in a saucepan and heat on medium high, stirring, until sauce begins to bubble. Remove and pour over pasta.

CHANGE IT UP

ADDITIONS
For a southwestern flavour, add 2 small cups of espresso to chili

Add 1 cup (250 mL) diced cooked chicken to make a hearty chicken chili

This is a surprisingly good meatless chili – sweet, savoury and healthy. If you want more heft, add textured vegetable protein, which looks like, and has the texture of, ground meat: you can find this in the vegetarian section of some grocery stores or in health food stores.

COUNTERTOP TO TABLE CUISINE

Rainbow Vegetable Rice with Fresh Basil

INGREDIENTS

$^1/_2$ medium red onion, peeled and coarsely chopped

$^1/_2$ sweet red pepper, seeded and coarsely chopped

$^1/_2$ green pepper, seeded and coarsely chopped

2 celery stalks, coarsely chopped

2 carrots, peeled and coarsely chopped

1 small tomato, chopped

2 cloves garlic, chopped OR $^1/_2$ tsp (2 mL) bottled minced garlic

2 tbsp chopped fresh basil

2 tbsp (30 mL) olive oil

1 cup (250 mL) long-grain white rice

2 cups (500 mL) vegetable stock

$^1/_2$ tsp (2 mL) sea salt

$^1/_2$ tsp (2 mL) black pepper

$^1/_4$ cup (50 mL) freshly grated Parmesan cheese, for garnish

SERVES 4

METHOD

1. In a blender or food processor, combine onion, peppers, celery, carrots, tomato, garlic and basil. Pulse or chop until vegetables are finely chopped and well combined.

2. Transfer to rice cooker and add oil, rice, stock, salt and pepper. Cover and allow to cook to perfection, about 18 to 20 minutes, or when the "warm" light illuminates.

3. Once the dish is ready, and still hot, sprinkle with Parmesan, mix lightly and serve.

The variety of vegetables in this recipe not only provides a pleasing taste, but also a multi-hued healthy meal.

CHANGE IT UP

VARIATION
If you don't have soup stock handy, just add the equivalent of water

ADDITION
Add 2 boneless and skinless chicken breasts with salt, pepper and basil on top. Steam while the rice is cooking.

SPICY
Add 1 jalapeno chili pepper, seeded and chopped

Apple Rice with Lamb & a Hint of Cinnamon

INGREDIENTS

1 small red onion, peeled and coarsely chopped

2 apples, cored and coarsely chopped

1 small sweet red pepper, seeded and coarsely chopped

2 tbsp (30 mL) olive oil

1 lb (450 g) stewing lamb, cut into $1/2$ inch (1.25 cm) cubes

$1/4$ cup (50 mL) raisins

$1/2$ tsp (2 mL) ground cinnamon

1 $1/2$ cups (375 mL) long-grain white rice

3 $1/2$ cups (875 mL) unsweetened apple juice

$1/2$ tbsp (10 mL) sea salt

1 tsp (5 mL) black pepper

SERVES 4 TO 6

METHOD

1. In a blender or food processor, combine onion, apples and red pepper. Set to pulse or chop until ingredients are finely chopped and well combined.

2. Transfer mixture to a rice cooker and add oil, lamb, raisins, cinnamon, rice, apple juice, salt and pepper.

3. Cover and allow to cook until "warm" light illuminates.

VEGETARIAN OPTION
Leave out the lamb and reduce the apple juice by 2 cups (500 mL) – serve as a side dish

The combination of lamb with apples – and raisins – makes this a delightfully sweet and savoury dish.

CHANGE IT UP

VARIATION
Substitute 1 cup (250 mL) coconut milk and half cup (125 mL) shredded, unsweetened coconut for apple juice and apples

ADDITION
Once cooked, add half cup (125 mL) crumbled feta cheese

Smoked Salmon with Orange & Grand Marnier Soup

INGREDIENTS

1 small red onion, peeled and coarsely chopped

1 small sweet red pepper, seeded and coarsely chopped

4 large carrots, peeled and grated

1 small orange, peeled and chopped

2 tbsp (30 mL) grated orange zest

2 cups (500 mL) chopped smoked salmon

4 cups (1 L) vegetable soup stock

2 tbsp (30 mL) Grand Marnier liqueur

$1/2$ tsp (2 mL) dried basil

$1/2$ tsp (2 mL) dried thyme

$1/2$ tsp (2 mL) sea salt

$1/2$ tsp (2 mL) black pepper

$1/2$ cup (125 mL) whipping cream

Although an unusual combination of flavours, the smoked salmon is well balanced by the carrot, orange and Grand Marnier. This soup is best served hot with an appetizer.

SERVES 4 TO 6

METHOD

1. In a blender or food processor, combine onion, red pepper, carrots and orange. Set to pulse or chop until vegetables and orange are finely chopped and well combined.

2. Transfer vegetable-orange mixture to rice cooker and add zest, salmon, stock, Grand Marnier, basil, thyme, salt and pepper. Cook until "warm" light is illuminated.

3. Using a hand blender, purée the soup while still in the rice cooker; add cream, mix well, and serve.

ACCOMPANIMENT TIP

As a wonderful side-dish or appetizer to the main meal, marinate 8 jumbo shrimp in a bowl of orange juice for approximately 1 hour. Once done, discard marinade and skewer shrimp in twos, lengthwise, on four skewers. Transfer skewers to rice cooker's steamer basket; steam for approximately 12 to 15 minutes or until shrimp is cooked. Place each skewer over soup bowl before serving.

CHANGE IT UP

VARIATION
Substitute smoked trout or 2 cups (500 mL) shrimp or crabmeat for smoked salmon

LOWER FAT OPTION
Substitute skim milk for whipping cream

Mushroom Soup Galore

INGREDIENTS

3 cups (750 mL) button mushrooms, coarsely chopped

4 medium portobello mushrooms, coarsely chopped

2 cloves garlic, chopped OR 1/2 tsp (2 mL) bottled minced garlic

1 small onion, peeled and coarsely chopped

4 cups (1 L) vegetable stock

1/2 tsp (2 mL) dried oregano

1/2 tsp (2 mL) dried sage

1/2 tsp (2 mL) sea salt

1/2 tsp (2 mL) black pepper

1/2 cup (125 mL) table cream

1/2 cup (125 mL) whipping cream

SERVES 4 TO 6

METHOD

1. In a blender or food processor, combine mushrooms, garlic and onion. Set to pulse or chop until vegetables are finely chopped and well combined.

2. Transfer the vegetable mixture to a rice cooker and add vegetable stock, oregano, sage, salt and pepper. Cover and cook until "warm" light illuminates.

3. Using a hand blender, purée the soup while still in rice cooker; add cream, mix well, and serve.

As the title suggests, this is a mushroom soup that doesn't skimp on the mushrooms.

CHANGE IT UP

VARIATION

To make a delicious broccoli cream soup, substitute mushrooms with 6 cups (1500 mL) chopped broccoli florets

LOWER FAT OPTION

Omit the cream and use 1 cup (250 mL) skim milk

Lazy Jambalaya

INGREDIENTS

1 small red onion, peeled and coarsely chopped

1 small green pepper, seeded and coarsely chopped

1 small sweet red pepper, seeded and coarsely chopped

3 cloves garlic, chopped OR 1 tsp (5 mL) bottled minced garlic

3 celery stalks, coarsely chopped

2 cups (500 mL) vegetable stock

3 tbsp (45 mL) olive oil

1 cup (250 mL) white rice

2 medium sweet Italian sausages, cooked and sliced

1 boneless, skinless chicken breast, cooked and cubed

1 14-oz (398 mL) can diced stewed tomatoes, undrained

1 tbsp (15 mL) chili powder

1/2 tsp (2 mL) dried basil OR 2 tbsp (15 mL) chopped fresh

1 tsp (5 mL) sea salt

1/2 tsp (2 mL) black pepper

1 bay leaf

2 cups (500 mL) raw medium shrimp, peeled and deveined

1/2 cup (125 mL) chopped fresh flat-leaf (Italian) parsley

CHANGE IT UP

ADDITION
Add freshly grated Parmesan cheese for even more flavour

LOWER FAT OPTION
Omit the olive oil

SPICY
Add 1 jalapeno chili pepper, seeded and chopped

SERVES 4 TO 6

METHOD

1. In a blender or food processor, combine onion, peppers, garlic and celery. Set to pulse or chop until vegetables are finely chopped and well combined.

2. Transfer vegetable mixture to rice cooker and add stock, oil, rice, sausages, chicken, tomatoes, chili powder, basil, salt, pepper and bay leaf. Cover and cook until the "warm" light illuminates, approximately 18 to 20 minutes.

3. Once done, remove the bay leaf and discard; add shrimp and parsley and mix with the rice. Cover and keep on warm for 5 minutes more before serving.

VEGETARIAN OPTION
Leave out sausage, chicken and shrimp. Add 3 sliced portobello mushrooms and 1 cup (250 mL) chopped firm tofu.

ENTERTAINING TIP
If you're having a "stand up" instead of a "sit down", you might want to try these roll-ups or rice balls:

To make roll-ups: In a soft tortilla shell, spoon jambalaya onto one end of each round. Sprinkle each rice mound liberally with grated cheddar cheese and roll, starting with the filling end. Place in a toaster oven and grill for 2 to 3 minutes or until roll-ups are slightly browned. Cut each roll-up into 4 and serve hot as hors d'oeuvres.

To make rice balls: Once jambalaya is prepared, allow to cool in refrigerator. When ready, remove and, using your hands, create bite-size balls and coat in flour. Fry in a deep fryer for 2 to 3 minutes or until slightly browned.

Espresso Basil Beef Stew with Red Wine & Dijon

INGREDIENTS

2 tbsp (30 mL) olive oil

1 lb (450 g) stewing beef, cubed

2 carrots, peeled and coarsely chopped

2 cloves garlic, chopped OR ½ tsp (2 mL) bottled minced garlic

3 celery stalks, coarsely chopped

1 small red onion, coarsely chopped

1 small sweet red pepper, seeded and coarsely chopped

1 small green pepper, seeded and coarsely chopped

3 medium potatoes, peeled and cubed

1 cup (250 mL) red wine

3 tbsp (45 mL) Dijon mustard

3 tbsp (45 mL) Worcestershire sauce

½ cup (125 mL) chopped fresh basil

4 cups (1 L) beef stock

2 small cups espresso

½ tsp (2 mL) sea salt

½ tsp (2 mL) black pepper

SERVES 4 TO 6

METHOD

1. In a rice cooker, add the olive oil and heat for a minute or two. Add the beef and sauté 4 to 5 minutes or until browned on all sides. Remove beef and set aside.

2. Meanwhile, in a blender or food processor, combine carrots, garlic, celery, onion and peppers. Set to pulse or chop until vegetables are finely chopped and well combined.

3. Transfer vegetable mixture to rice cooker and add beef, potatoes, red wine, mustard, Worcestershire sauce, basil, beef stock, espresso, salt and pepper. Cover and allow to cook until "warm" light illuminates, approximately 18 to 20 minutes.

VEGETARIAN OPTION
Replace beef with large sliced portobello mushrooms and beef stock with vegetable stock

This coffee-flavoured basil beef stew was inspired by my Argentinian friend, Paco, who while we sipped espresso in a café close to the Via Veneto, extolled the virtues of his country's exceptional vineyards and beef. Pairing red wine with beef is not so unusual of course – but accentuating it with espresso certainly sets it apart from other stews.

CHANGE IT UP

VARIATIONS
Substitute beef with stewing lamb and basil with half cup (50 mL) chopped fresh rosemary

Leave out potatoes and add 1 cup (250 mL) rice or barley

ADDITION
Add pitted, black olives and crumbled feta cheese just before serving

LOWER FAT OPTION
Omit olive oil and drain beef before returning to rice cooker

SPICY
Add 1 tbsp (15 mL) hot sauce during step 3

Bowl Handle Position

Lock

Unlock

Oster

FOOD PROCESSOR

Cooking is fun!

Slicing, dicing, mixing, and other tedious food preparation isn't necessarily fun. But with a versatile and powerful food processor you get to have all the fun, and the appliance does all the hard work. With these recipes the results are delicious, but to do all the prep work by hand would take more time than most people have for meal preparation. All these dishes were mixed in minutes, and the multiple speed motor with "pulse" option delivered perfect consistency every time. It's great when the appliance does the work and I can take the credit.

Carrot & Raisin Salad with Fennel

INGREDIENTS

6 medium carrots, peeled and chopped

1 fennel bulb, chopped

1/2 cup (125 mL) chopped green onion

1/2 cup (125 mL) mayonnaise

1/4 cup (60 mL) table cream

2 tbsp (30 mL) olive oil

2 tbsp (30 mL) balsamic vinegar

2 tbsp (30 mL) granulated sugar OR liquid honey

1/2 tsp (2 mL) dried mint OR 2 tbsp chopped fresh mint

1/2 tsp (2 mL) sea salt

1/2 tsp (2 mL) white pepper

1/2 cup (125 mL) raisins

SERVES 2 TO 4

METHOD

1. In a food processor, combine carrots, fennel and green onion. Process until vegetables are grated and well mixed.

2. Add mayonnaise, cream, oil, balsamic vinegar, sugar, mint, salt and pepper. Continue processing until well mixed. If too dry, add more mayonnaise.

3. Transfer to a medium bowl, add raisins and mix well. Refrigerate, covered, at least 2 hours prior to serving.

The addition of fennel in this salad elevates it from the ordinary to the extraordinarily delicious. Serve this with herbed rice cooked in orange-flavoured water, and with mint-and-honey-glazed chicken breasts.

CHANGE IT UP

VARIATION
Substitute half cup (125 mL) dried cranberries or chopped dried apricots for raisins

ADDITION
Add 1 cup (250 mL) cooked, cubed chicken

LOWER FAT OPTION
Use non-fat or light mayonnaise

Quick & Easy Strawberry Pie

INGREDIENTS

2 9-inch (22.5 cm) unbaked pie shells

4 cups (1 L) strawberries

1 cup (250 mL) granulated sugar

$1/3$ cup (75 mL) all-purpose flour

2 tbsp (30 mL) strawberry jam

4 tsp (20 mL) unsalted butter, softened

MAKES one 9 inch pie

METHOD

1. In a food processor, combine strawberries, sugar, flour and jam. Process until well mixed.

2. Transfer strawberry mixture into one pie shell and dot with butter.

3. Cover pie with other shell and make a slit in center with a knife to allow steam to escape.

3. Bake in a toaster oven, or oven on middle rack, at 425°F (220°C) for 10 minutes. Reduce to 350°F (175°C) and bake for another 20 minutes or until crust is golden brown.

This simple, easy pie – requiring very little preparation, and a food processor – is something I serve with frozen strawberry yogurt or ice cream. If you want a quick and easy bumbleberry pie, just substitute 3 of the 4 cups of strawberries for berries of your choice.

CHANGE IT UP

VARIATION

Substitute 4 cups (1 L) blueberries or raspberries for strawberries and blueberry or raspberry jam for strawberry jam

LOWER FAT OPTION

Instead of sugar, use a low-calorie sweetener suitable for baking

Gazpacho Soup with Coriander

INGREDIENTS

2 carrots, peeled and chopped

1 small red onion, peeled and chopped

2 cloves garlic, chopped

1 small English cucumber, chopped

1 small sweet red pepper, seeded and chopped

1 small green pepper, seeded and chopped

1 cup (250 mL) cauliflower florets

1 cup (250 mL) broccoli florets

1 19-oz (540 mL) can stewed tomatoes, undrained

1 cup (250 mL) tomato juice

4 cups (1 L) vegetable stock

1/2 cup (125 mL) chopped fresh coriander

1 tbsp (15 mL) granulated sugar OR liquid honey

1 tsp (5 mL) chili powder

1 tsp (5 mL) paprika

1/2 tsp (2 mL) sea salt

1 tsp (5 mL) black pepper

SERVES 4 TO 6

METHOD

1. In a food processor, combine carrots, onion, garlic, cucumber, peppers, cauliflower, broccoli and tomatoes. Process until vegetables are finely chopped.

2. Transfer to a large bowl, add tomato juice, vegetable stock, coriander, sugar, chili powder, paprika, salt and pepper and, using a wooden spoon, mix well.

3. Refrigerate, covered with plastic wrap, for 2 hours prior to serving.

Gazpacho is a Spanish soup served cold – often chilled with ice cubes when consumed in southern Spain during the unbearably hot summer months. The Spanish thicken their gazpacho with day-old bread; my version omits the bread but is thick with vegetables. Serve this with garnishes of finely chopped cucumber, tomatoes, red onion and croutons.

CHANGE IT UP

VARIATIONS

Heat 2 cups (500 mL) of gazpacho and use as a pasta sauce

Use gazpacho as a poaching liquid for fish or chicken

Use 1 cup (250 mL) gazpacho in rice cooker to add flavour to rice dish

SPICY

Add 1 tsp (5 mL) cayenne pepper

Baked Apple Pancake

INGREDIENTS

4 eggs

1 cup (250 mL) milk

1$\frac{1}{2}$ cup (375 mL) all-purpose flour

2 tbsp (30 mL) granulated sugar

$\frac{1}{4}$ cup (50 mL) applesauce

$\frac{1}{2}$ apple, peeled and cored

$\frac{1}{4}$ tsp (1 mL) ground cinnamon

MAKES one 8-inch pancake SERVES 4

METHOD

1. In a food processor, combine milk, flour, eggs, applesauce, apple, sugar and cinnamon. Process until mixture forms a batter.

2. Transfer batter into a greased 8 x 8-inch (20 x 20 cm) cake pan.

3. Bake in the oven at 350°F (175°C) for 15 to 18 minutes. Insert a toothpick or knife in the center; if toothpick comes out clean, pancake is ready.

Baked in the oven, this is a delicious pancake that requires minimal preparation: just throw everything into the food processor and then the oven. Serve for breakfast or brunch with maple syrup, sliced apples, applesauce or a dollop of yogurt on top.

CHANGE IT UP

VARIATIONS

Make individual pancakes in a skillet

Use small, foil-lined deep pot pie plates to make smaller pancakes, bake for 12 to 15 minutes

Ken's Homemade Tartar Sauce with Red Pepper & Dijon

INGREDIENTS

2 medium dill pickles, coarsely chopped

$1/2$ small sweet red pepper, seeded and coarsely chopped

$1/2$ small red onion, peeled and coarsely chopped

$1/4$ cup (50 mL) chopped fresh parsley

$3/4$ cup (175 mL) mayonnaise

2 tbsp (30 mL) table cream

1 tbsp (15 mL) Dijon mustard

1 tbsp (15 mL) balsamic vinegar

1 tsp (5 mL) granulated sugar OR liquid honey

MAKES approximately 1 TO $1^1/_2$ cups

METHOD

1. In a food processor, combine pickles, red pepper, onion and parsley. Process until mixture is chopped fine and well mixed.

2. Add mayonnaise, cream, Dijon mustard, balsamic vinegar and sugar. Continue processing until smooth.

3. Transfer to bowl, cover with plastic wrap and refrigerate for 2 hours to blend the flavours.

Serve this with battered fish or chilled vegetable crudités.

CHANGE IT UP

VARIATIONS

To use as a salad dressing, combine quarter cup (50 mL) tartar sauce, half cup (125 mL) olive oil and 2 tbsp (30 mL) vinegar and mix well.

SPICY

Add 1 jalapeno chili pepper, seeded and chopped to the mixture

COUNTERTOP TO TABLE CUISINE

The Best Pesto

INGREDIENTS

1$\frac{1}{2}$ cup (125 mL) olive oil

$\frac{3}{4}$ cup (175 mL) chopped fresh basil

$\frac{1}{4}$ cup (50 mL) pine nuts

$\frac{1}{4}$ cup (50 mL) freshly grated Parmesan cheese OR pecorino cheese

$\frac{1}{4}$ cup (50 mL) balsamic vinegar

2 cloves garlic, chopped OR 1 tsp (5 mL) bottled minced garlic

2 anchovy fillets OR $\frac{1}{2}$ tsp (2 mL) anchovy paste

1 tsp (5 mL) Dijon mustard

$\frac{1}{2}$ tsp (2 mL) sea salt

$\frac{1}{2}$ tsp (2 mL) black pepper

MAKES **2 TO 3** cups

METHOD

1. In a food processor, combine oil, basil, pine nuts, Parmesan cheese, balsamic vinegar, garlic, anchovies, Dijon mustard, salt and pepper. Process until mixture resembles a paste.

2. Serve with pasta or vegetables at room temperature. If using later, transfer to a covered container and chill. It will keep for up to a week, tightly covered, stored in the refrigerator, or for a few months in the freezer.

Traditional pesto, the recipe for which originated in Genoa, Italy, is made with basil, pine nuts, Parmesan cheese, garlic and oil. What makes this pesto "besto", and pleasantly piquant, is the introduction of anchovies, Dijon mustard and balsamic vinegar. Toss this with pasta, steamed or cooked vegetables, or mixed in with rice.

CHANGE IT UP

VARIATION

To make "red pesto", substitute 2 small sweet red peppers, seeded, roasted and chopped, for the fresh basil

LOWER FAT OPTION

Substitute half cup (125 mL) chicken stock for olive oil

Roasted Red Pepper & Walnut Dip

INGREDIENTS

4 medium sweet red peppers, seeded and coarsely chopped

1 small onion, coarsely chopped

2 cloves garlic, chopped

2 tbsp (30 mL) olive oil

1 cup (250 mL) sour cream

1/4 cup (50 mL) whipping cream

1/2 cup (125 mL) walnut pieces

2 tbsp (30 mL) balsamic vinegar

2 tbsp (30 mL) liquid honey

1/2 tsp (2 mL) dried basil

1/2 tsp (2 mL) sea salt

1/2 tsp (2 mL) white pepper

MAKES 2 TO 3 cups

METHOD

1. In a food processor, combine peppers, onion and garlic. Process until chopped fine.

2. In a skillet, heat oil. Transfer vegetable mixture to skillet and sauté for 4 to 5 minutes or until peppers are tender.

3. Return sautéed vegetables to food processor and add sour cream, whipping cream, walnuts, balsamic vinegar, honey, basil, salt and pepper. Process until smooth.

4. Transfer dip to a bowl and refrigerate, covered in plastic wrap, at least 2 hours prior to serving.

You can serve this as a dip, or as a spread on toast or foccacia.

CHANGE IT UP

VARIATION

This makes a great pasta sauce: in a saucepan, slowly heat on a medium-low setting and serve with cooked pasta

LOWER FAT OPTION

Substitute non-fat sour cream for sour cream

Substitute skim milk for whipping cream

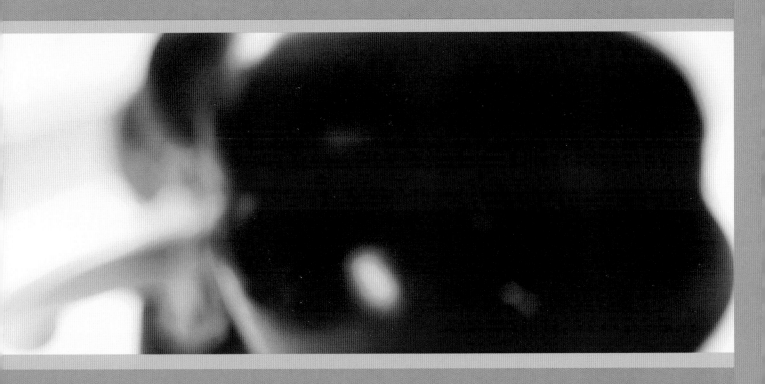

Black Bean Dip with Cilantro & Garlic

INGREDIENTS

1 small red onion, peeled and chopped

2 cloves garlic, chopped OR 1 tsp (5 mL) bottled minced garlic

1/2 cup (125 mL) chopped fresh coriander

1 19-oz (540 mL) can black beans, rinsed and drained

1 tbsp (15 mL) tomato paste

1/2 cup (125 mL) sour cream

1/2 tsp (2 mL) sea salt

1/2 tsp (2 mL) black pepper

1/2 tsp (2 mL) cayenne pepper

MAKES approximately 2 cups

METHOD

1. In a food processor, combine onion, garlic and coriander. Process until finely chopped and well mixed.

2. Add beans, tomato, paste, sour cream, cayenne, salt and pepper. Continue processing until smooth and creamy. If dip is too thick, add more sour cream or a bit of olive oil and process.

This is a creamy alternative to hummus. Serve this with whole-wheat pita triangles, brushed with oil, sprinkled with cayenne, and baked in the oven until just crispy.

CHANGE IT UP

VARIATION
Substitute chick peas for black beans to make a spicy variation of hummus

LOWER FAT OPTION
Substitute non-fat sour cream for sour cream

COUNTERTOP TO TABLE CUISINE

ELECTRIC SKILLET

Sizzilin'!

One of the best things about cooking in this skillet is the small amount of olive oil required and with the Inspire® Electric Skillet excess oil is drained through the special lift technology for a healthier, less heavy taste. A skillet can also be used to prepare some delicious "poached" dishes such as my Poached Cranberry Chicken with Red Wine. The electric skillet replaces your frying or sauté pan and consumes far less energy than a stovetop burner. The dishwasher safe components and non-stick surface make clean up a snap. When it comes to fried foods, moderation is the key – and total abstinence is...boring!

Three-Cheese Casserole in a Skillet with Herbs & Tomato
Sole of Ouzo with Fennel
Poached Cranberry Chicken with Red Wine
Tofu & Beans with Tomatoes & Red Wine
Marmalade-Glazed Shrimp Stir-Fry
Vegetable Stir-Fry with Mandarin Oranges & Honey
Spicy Beef in an Herbed Red Wine Tomato Sauce
Breaded Pork Chops with Tarragon & Lemon

Three-Cheese Casserole in a Skillet with Herbs & Tomato

INGREDIENTS

1 small red onion, peeled and coarsely chopped

1 small sweet red pepper, seeded and coarsely chopped

1 medium zucchini, coarsely chopped

1 carrot, peeled and coarsely chopped

1 28-oz (796 mL) can diced tomatoes, undrained

1/2 tsp (2 mL) sea salt

1/2 tsp (2 mL) black pepper

1/2 tsp (2 mL) dried basil

1/2 tsp (2 mL) dried thyme

3 cups (750 mL) vegetable stock

2 cups (500 mL) macaroni shells

1/2 cup (125 mL) shredded cheddar cheese

1/4 cup (50 mL) grated Parmesan cheese

1/2 cup (125 mL) shredded Swiss cheese

SERVES 4 TO 6

METHOD

1. In a blender or food processor, combine onion, red pepper, zucchini and carrots. Set to pulse and/or chop until vegetables are finely chopped and well mixed.

2. Set the electric skillet to 450°F (230°C). Transfer the vegetable mixture to skillet and add tomatoes, salt, pepper, basil, thyme, stock and macaroni. Cook 7 to 8 minutes or until the macaroni is tender.

3. Add the cheese and mix well. Reduce heat to simmer, and cook, covered, for another 2 to 3 minutes or until cheese is melted.

This macaroni-and-cheese extravaganza is a meal in itself. Tasty and filling, you can offset with a mixed green salad and/or a carrot or squash soup on the side.

CHANGE IT UP

VARIATION
Replace Swiss cheese with Gruyere or Fontina, or whichever you prefer

ADDITION
Add 2 cups cooked chicken or beef

Sole of Ouzo with Fennel

INGREDIENTS

4 garlic cloves, chopped OR 2 tsp (10 mL) bottled minced garlic

1 small sweet red pepper, seeded and coarsely chopped

1 small red onion, coarsely chopped

1 small fennel bulb, coarsely chopped

3 tbsp (45 mL) olive oil

2 oz (56 mL) Ouzo liqueur

$1/2$ cup (125 mL) unsweetened apple juice

2 tbsp (30 mL) freshly squeezed lemon juice

$1/2$ tsp (2 mL) black pepper

$1/2$ tsp (2 mL) sea salt

4 8-oz sole fillets

SERVES 2 TO 4

METHOD

1. In a blender or food processor, combine garlic, red pepper, onion and fennel. Set to pulse and/or chop for 1 minute or until well mixed.

2. Heat the oil in an electric skillet at 450°F (230°C). Transfer the vegetable mixture to skillet and add Ouzo liqueur, apple juice, lemon juice, salt and pepper. Sauté for 5 to 6 minutes or until fennel is tender.

3. Add sole and reduce heat to simmer. Continue cooking for another 5 to 6 minutes or until the sole turns an opaque white.

VEGETARIAN OPTION

Substitute 4 large portobello mushrooms, stems removed, for sole

This Greek-inspired dish serves up a double-whammy of anise from the Ouzo and the fennel, also known as "sweet anise". The licorice-flavoured anise complements the sole, never overpowering it. If you do serve this at a dinner party, be certain to have enough Ouzo to savour as an aperitif.

CHANGE IT UP

VARIATION
Substitute the sole with 4 large (8 to 10-oz) red snapper fillets

LOWER FAT OPTION
Omit the olive oil when sautéing the vegetables

Poached Cranberry Chicken with Red Wine

INGREDIENTS

2 tbsp (30 mL) olive oil

1 small red onion, peeled and coarsely chopped

1 small sweet red pepper, seeded and coarsely chopped

2 cloves garlic, coarsely chopped OR $^1/_2$ tsp (2 mL) bottled minced garlic

3 cups (750 mL) cranberry juice

$^1/_2$ cup (125 mL) dry red wine

$^1/_2$ tsp (2 mL) dried basil

$^1/_2$ tsp (2 mL) dried thyme

$^1/_2$ tsp (2 mL) sea salt

$^1/_2$ tsp (2 mL) black pepper

1 cup (250 mL) dried cranberries

4 boneless, skinless chicken breasts

SERVES 4 TO 6

METHOD

1. In a blender or food processor, combine onion, red pepper and garlic. Set to pulse or chop for 1 minute or until vegetables are well mixed.

2. Set electric skillet at 400°F (205°C) and add oil. Once oil is heated, transfer vegetable mixture and sauté for 2 to 3 minutes or until onion is translucent. Add juice, wine, basil, thyme, salt and pepper. When liquid begins to boil, reduce to a simmer.

3. Add the chicken and cover. Poach for about 15 to 18 minutes, turning breasts every five minutes.

4. When ready to serve, reserve some of the poaching liquid and spoon over breasts.

ENTERTAINING TIP
Thinly slice the poached chicken breasts and serve on a platter with toothpicks and drizzled sauce

This is an extremely delicious and healthy recipe to serve to dinner guests. I sometimes slice the chicken breasts and serve on a bed of greens – arugula being the preferred green.

CHANGE IT UP

VARIATIONS

To make Poached Raspberry Chicken: Substitute 3 cups raspberry juice for cranberry juice and 1 cup thawed frozen raspberries for dried cranberries

Substitute 4 to 6-oz swordfish or tuna steaks for chicken

Substitute the red wine with a non-fat chicken stock

Tofu & Beans with Tomatoes & Red Wine

INGREDIENTS

2 cloves garlic, chopped OR 1 tsp (5 mL) bottled minced garlic

1 small red onion, coarsely chopped

1 small red pepper, seeded and coarsely chopped

1 small green pepper, seeded and coarsely chopped

1/2 cup (125 mL) chopped fresh coriander

2 tbsp (30 mL) olive oil

1 lb (450 mL) firm tofu, cut into 1/2-inch cubes

1/2 cup (125 mL) red wine

1 28-oz (796 mL) can diced tomatoes, undrained

1 19-oz (540 mL) can mixed beans, rinsed and drained

2 tbsp (30 mL) balsamic vinegar

1 tsp (5 mL) chili powder

1 tsp (5 mL) dried basil

1/2 tsp (2 mL) sea salt

1/2 tsp (2 mL) black pepper

SERVES 6

METHOD

1. In a blender or food processor, combine garlic, onion, peppers and coriander. Set to pulse and/or chop until well mixed.

2. Heat oil in an electric skillet at 450°F (230°C) and sauté tofu for about 2 to 3 minutes or until browned.

3. Transfer vegetable mixture to skillet and continue sautéing for another 3 to 4 minutes.

4. Add red wine and allow the alcohol to burn off, about 2 minutes.

5. Next, add tomatoes, beans, balsamic vinegar, chili powder, basil, salt and pepper; allow to cook for another 12 to 15 minutes at 300°F (150°C).

The delicate-flavoured tofu, coming together with a medley of beans and seasoned with herbs, tomatoes, balsamic vinegar and red wine, will convert any carnivore to the vegetarian way.

CHANGE IT UP

VARIATIONS

Replace the tofu with 2 chicken breasts, sliced or 18 large shrimp

To make a hearty chili, replace the tofu with 1 lb (450 mL) ground beef

Replace coriander with Italian (also known as flat-leaf) parsley

SPICY

Add 1 jalapeno pepper, seeded and finely chopped (wear gloves when seeding and chopping jalapeno, to avoid contact with your skin) to step 1

Marmalade-Glazed Shrimp Stir-Fry

INGREDIENTS

3 tbsp (45 mL) olive oil

24 large shrimp

2 cloves garlic, chopped

1 small red onion, thinly sliced

2 carrots, peeled and thinly sliced

1 sweet red pepper, seeded and thinly sliced

1 cup (250 mL) broccoli florets

1 cup (250 mL) cauliflower florets

1 tbsp (15 mL) minced ginger

1/2 tsp (2 mL) dried basil

1/2 tsp (2 mL) dried thyme

1/2 cup (125 mL) orange marmalade

1/4 cup (50 mL) soy sauce

SERVES 4

METHOD

1. Set the electric skillet to 400°F (205°C) and add oil. When oil is heated, add shrimp and sauté for 4 to 5 minutes or until shrimp are pink.

2. Add garlic, onion, carrots, pepper, broccoli, cauliflower, ginger, basil and thyme; continue sautéing for 10 to 12 minutes.

3. Add the marmalade and soy sauce and mix well. Reduce heat and simmer for 2 to 3 minutes.

4. Once ready, turn off heat, remove from skillet and serve stir-fry on a bed of greens, fragrant rice, or rice noodles.

VEGETARIAN OPTION

Replace the shrimp with 5 portobello mushrooms, sliced half-inch thick.

This is one of the best stir-fries in my repertoire. Although the recipe calls for orange marmalade, if you can find ginger marmalade or carrot marmalade, don't hesitate to use it instead.

CHANGE IT UP

VARIATION
Substitute 2 cups (500 mL) scallops or cooked sliced chicken for shrimp

ADDITION
Add cooked oriental noodles to skillet and mix well

LOWER FAT OPTION
Leave out the olive oil

SPICY
Add 1 tsp (5 mL) hot sauce to skillet when shrimp are simmering

Vegetable Stir-Fry with Mandarin Oranges & Honey

INGREDIENTS

3 tbsp (45 mL) olive oil

1 red onion, sliced

1 sweet red pepper, seeded and sliced in thin strips

1 green pepper, seeded and sliced in thin strips

2 medium carrots, sliced diagonally, 1/4 inch thick

2 portobello mushrooms, sliced in thin strips

1 cup (250 mL) broccoli florets

2 celery stalks, sliced diagonally

1/2 tsp (2 mL) minced, peeled fresh ginger

1/4 cup (50 mL) orange juice

1 cup (250 mL) canned mandarin orange segments, drained

2 tbsp (30 mL) orange marmalade

1/2 cup (125 mL) liquid honey

1/4 cup (50 mL) soy sauce

1/2 tsp (2 mL) black pepper

SERVES 4

METHOD

1. Set an electric skillet to 450°F (230°C) and add oil. When oil is heated, add onion, peppers, carrots, mushrooms, broccoli, celery and ginger. Stir fry for 5 minutes or until carrots are tender.

2. Reduce heat to 300°F (150°C) and add juice, orange segments, marmalade, honey, soy sauce and pepper. Cook for about 3 to 5 minutes more.

3. Mix well and serve immediately.

I never tire of sweetening the pot! In this stir-fry the vegetables are underscored with a stand-out combination of marmalade, sweet mandarin orange and honey. Serve it on a bed of fragrant rice, garnish with sprigs of coriander and accompany it with a baby spinach salad.

CHANGE IT UP

ADDITION
Add shrimp or chicken to recipe

LOWER FAT OPTION
Substitute low-calorie marmalade for marmalade

Replace olive oil with non-fat vegetable stock to sauté

Spicy Beef with Red Wine in an Herbed Tomato Sauce

INGREDIENTS

1 small red onion, coarsely chopped

3 cloves garlic, chopped OR 1½ tsp (7 mL) bottled minced garlic

1 small sweet red pepper, seeded and coarsely chopped

1 small green pepper, seeded and coarsely chopped

1 jalapeno chili pepper, seeded and chopped

3 tbsp (45 mL) olive oil

1 lb (450 mL) top sirloin, sliced into strips

1 cup (250 mL) red wine

2 tbsp (30 mL) chopped fresh rosemary OR 1 tsp (5 mL) dried

2 tbsp (30 mL) chopped fresh basil OR 1 tsp (5 mL) dried

1 19-oz (540 mL) can diced tomatoes, undrained

½ tsp (2 mL) sea salt

½ tsp (2 mL) black pepper

SERVES 4

METHOD

1. In a blender or food processor, combine onion, garlic and peppers. Set to pulse and/or chop for 1 minute or until well mixed.

2. Heat the oil in the electric skillet at 450°F (230°C). Add beef and sauté for 4 to 5 minutes, turning often. Add vegetable mixture and sauté another 3 to 4 minutes. Add the wine and allow the alcohol to reduce, all the while mixing, for about 2 to 3 minutes.

3. Add rosemary, basil, tomatoes, salt and pepper. Sauté at 350°F (175°C) for a few minutes then return lid and allow to cook for about about 8 to 10 minutes.

VEGETARIAN OPTION
Substitute the beef with 6 large portobello mushrooms, sliced ½ inch thick

What makes this beef so deliciously spicy-hot is the addition of a jalapeno chili pepper. If you don't have jalapeno, substitute with half teaspoon cayenne pepper.

CHANGE IT UP

VARIATION
Replace beef with chicken strips or shrimp

LOWER FAT OPTION
Omit the oil and use a lean-cut beef such as a tenderloin

COUNTERTOP TO TABLE CUISINE

Breaded Pork Chops with Tarragon & Lemon

INGREDIENTS

1/2 cup (125 mL) dried bread crumbs

1 tbsp (15 mL) dried tarragon

1 tsp (5 mL) cornstarch

1 tsp (5 mL) paprika

1/2 tsp (2 mL) garlic powder

1/2 tsp (2 mL) onion powder

1/2 tsp (2 mL) sea salt

1/2 tsp (2 mL) black pepper

1 large egg

4 pork chops

2 tbsp (30 mL) olive oil

2 lemons, cut into wedges, for garnish

SERVES 4

METHOD

1. In a medium mixing bowl, combine bread crumbs, tarragon, cornstarch, paprika, garlic powder, onion powder, salt and pepper; mix well and set aside.

2. In a separate bowl, beat egg with fork. Using tongs, dip each pork chop in egg, then coat both sides in bread-crumb mixture. If necessary, use a spoon to help cover both sides.

3. Set electric skillet at 350°F (175°C) or medium heat and add oil. When oil is heated, add breaded chops and cook each side for 5 to 6 minutes or until golden.

4. Remove chops from skillet, garnish with lemon slices, and serve.

Although this dish reminds me of comfort food, the addition of tarragon, garlic and lemon elevates these breaded chops on the culinary scale.

CHANGE IT UP

VARIATION
Replace the pork chops with veal chops, chicken or fish such as cod or sole

LOWER FAT OPTION
Substitute bread crumbs for half cup (125 mL) flour

SPICY
Add half tsp (2 mL) cayenne pepper to the dry mixture

BASKET WITH LID REMOVED

Oster

DEEP FRYER

Fit to be fried!

We all know that deep fried foods should be eaten in moderation, and I agree completely.
Still there are some foods that are so delicious when cooked in the fryer that it would be
a sin to do without them completely. The secret to healthier deep fryer cooking is to use
canola or vegetable oils, change the oil for each new dish, and keep the temperature as
low as possible. The Oster® Deep Fryer makes temperature control completely
automatic. It also reduces odors, splatters and makes clean up a snap.

These are some of my favourite deep-fried recipes and they make my dog, Napoleon
especially happy because he knows we'll be taking an extra long walk to burn off the
calories after dinner.

Red Wine Individual Ribs with Garlic & Herbs
Herbed Tempura Vegetables
Espresso Cinnamon Onion Rings
Spicy Southern-Fried Chicken
Crispy Chicken Fingers
Cajun Crusty Calamari
Ken's Beer Batter Fish
Chili Fries
Sweet Potato Frites with Cinnamon

Red Wine Individual Ribs with Garlic & Herbs

INGREDIENTS

3 lbs (1350 g) slab ribs, split into individual rib pieces

Vegetable oil for deep frying

MARINADE

2 cups (500 mL) dry red wine

4 cloves garlic, chopped OR 2 tsp (10 mL) bottled minced garlic

1 tsp (5 mL) dried basil

1 tsp (5 mL) dried thyme

1 tsp (5 mL) sea salt

1 tsp (5 mL) black pepper

DRY MIXTURE

2 tbsp (30 mL) garlic powder

2 tbsp (30 mL) dried basil

2 tbsp (30 mL) dried thyme

1 tbsp (15 mL) dried sage

1 tsp (5 mL) fine sea salt

1 tsp (5 mL) white pepper

SERVES 4 TO 6

METHOD

1. Using a rice cooker with water, cover and boil ribs for 10 minutes. Remove, drain and set aside.

2. In a blender, combine wine, garlic, basil, thyme, salt and pepper. Blend until marinade is well mixed. Transfer to a bowl or large resealable freezer bag and add the boiled ribs. Marinate, covered or sealed and refrigerated, overnight or for at least 4 to 8 hours prior to frying.

3. When ribs are marinated, heat oil in an electric deep fryer set to 375°F (190°C).

4. In a medium bowl, combine garlic powder, basil, thyme, sage, salt and pepper; mix well. Remove ribs from marinade and place on wax paper. Sprinkle dry mixture on the ribs, turning, so that all sides are evenly coated. Transfer ribs to deep-fryer basket, filling two-thirds of the way up, and fry 12 to 15 minutes or until ribs are cooked and golden. Remove, drain on paper towels, and serve.

ENTERTAINING TIP
Serve individual ribs with chutney or plum sauce for dipping

CHANGE IT UP

VARIATION
Substitute 3 lbs chicken wings or shrimp, for ribs. When using fish or shrimp, reduce cooking time to 8 to 10 minutes.

LOWER FAT OPTION
Use toaster oven and broil ribs for 18 to 20 minutes instead of deep frying

Herbed Tempura Vegetables

INGREDIENTS

Vegetable oil for deep frying

1 cup (250 mL) medium button mushrooms

20 fresh green beans, cleaned

2 medium sweet red peppers, seeded and chopped into large pieces

1 cup (250 mL) cauliflower or broccoli florets

1 egg

1 1/2 cups (375 mL) iced water

2 cups (500 mL) all-purpose flour

1/2 tsp (2 mL) dried basil

1/2 tsp (2 mL) dried thyme

1/2 tsp (2 mL) dried rosemary

1/2 tsp (2 mL) sea salt

SERVES 3 TO 4

METHOD

1. Heat oil in an electric deep fryer, set to 340°F (170°C).

2. To make tempura batter: in a food processor, combine egg, water, flour, basil, thyme, rosemary and salt. Process until smooth. Add vegetables, a small amount at a time, and coat with tempura batter.

3. Place vegetables into the deep fryer basket once the "ready" green light is on. To avoid crowding the vegetables, fry in several small batches. Fry 8 to 10 minutes or until battered vegetables are golden brown.

Tempura is a Japanese-style of battered and fried vegetables that is absolutely delicious. Serve these with soy sauce for dipping, and as an appetizer or entrée.

CHANGE IT UP

VARIATIONS

Use other vegetables such as chopped zucchini, eggplant, mushrooms or carrots

Use shrimp or chicken

COUNTERTOP TO TABLE CUISINE

Espresso Cinnamon Onion Rings

INGREDIENTS

Vegetable oil for deep frying

2 cups (500 mL) all-purpose flour

1½ cups (375 mL) cold water

½ cup (125 mL) espresso coffee

1 large egg

1 tsp (5 mL) cinnamon

½ tsp (2 mL) sea salt

½ tsp (2 mL) white pepper

4 large onions, peeled and sliced into ½ inch (1.25 cm) rings

SERVES 4 TO 6

METHOD

1. Heat oil in an electric deep fryer set to 340°F (170°C).

2. To make batter: in a food processor, combine flour, water, coffee, egg, cinnamon, salt and pepper. Process until well mixed.

3. Dip the onion rings into the batter and transfer to deep fryer basket, filling to only two-thirds. Cook the onion rings at 375°F (190°C) for 8 to 10 minutes or until rings are crispy and golden.

4. Remove, drain on paper towels, and serve.

These crispy coffee-and-cinnamon-flavoured onion rings are fabulous with blue-cheese topped burgers and beer.

CHANGE IT UP

VARIATION

For a more exotic flavour, omit the cinnamon and add 1 tbsp (15 mL) mild curry powder. Serve with fresh coriander and yogurt on the side for dipping.

SPICY

Omit the cinnamon and add 1 tsp (5 mL) cayenne pepper to batter

Spicy Southern-Fried Chicken

INGREDIENTS

Vegetable oil for deep frying

1 cup (250 mL) all-purpose flour

1 tsp (5 mL) cornstarch

2 tbsp (30 mL) paprika

2 tbsp (30 mL) chili powder

1 tsp (5 mL) cayenne pepper

1 tsp (5 mL) dried basil

$1/2$ tsp (2 mL) sea salt

$1/2$ tsp (2 mL) black pepper

4 eggs

2 fryer chickens, cut into serving pieces

SERVES 4 TO 6

METHOD

1. Heat oil in an electric deep fryer set to 340°F (170°C).

2. In a blender, combine flour, cornstarch, paprika, chili powder, cayenne pepper, basil, salt and pepper. Mix well and transfer to a shallow dish.

3. In another bowl, lightly beat eggs. Dip chicken pieces, one at a time, in egg and then dredge in the flour mixture, making sure all sides are well coated. Set chicken pieces aside on wax paper until all are done.

4. Carefully transfer 3 to 4 chicken pieces at at time into the deep fryer basket. Fry for 15 minutes or until golden. Remove, drain on paper towels, and serve.

I love southern-fried chicken, particularly when it's accompanied by fried green tomatoes and a sweet potato salad. Another terrific accompaniment to serve with, or on top of, this chicken is salsa: try something unusual, such as a pineapple and papaya salsa.

CHANGE IT UP

VARIATIONS

Substitute halibut for chicken and cook 8 to 10 minutes

Use chicken wings and cook 10 to 12 minutes

SPICY

Add more cayenne to the mixture

Crispy Chicken Fingers

INGREDIENTS

2 skinless, boneless chicken breasts, cut into 1-inch strips

2 cups (500 mL) milk

Vegetable oil for deep frying

4 cups (1 L) corn flakes

1½ cups (375 mL) all-purpose flour

1 tbsp (15 mL) cornstarch

1 tsp (5 mL) sea salt

1 tsp (5 mL) black pepper

1 tbsp (15 mL) chili powder

1 tsp (5 mL) paprika

1 tbsp (15 mL) garlic powder

2 eggs

SERVES 4

METHOD

1. In a medium bowl, combine chicken strips and milk. Cover, refrigerate and allow to soak overnight or for at least 4 to 6 hours prior to frying.

2. When chicken strips are ready, heat oil in an electric deep fryer set to 340°F (170°C).

3. Meanwhile, in a blender combine corn flakes, flour, cornstarch, salt, pepper, chili powder, paprika and garlic powder. Pulse until mixture is blended fine. Transfer dry mixture to a bowl and set aside.

4. In another bowl, lightly beat eggs. Dip chicken strips, one at a time, into egg and then dredge in the crumb mixture, making sure strips are well coated. Transfer to deep fryer basket and fry for 13 to 15 minutes or until strips are crispy and golden. Remove, drain on paper towels, and serve.

With an electric deep fryer, it's great to make your own chicken fingers. These are much spicier, and crisper, than the frozen variety. Do note that the chicken strips require marinating hours before frying: from 4 to 8 hours in advance, or you can marinate overnight, if you wish.

CHANGE IT UP

VARIATIONS

Substitute chicken wings for chicken breasts

Substitute halibut or cod for chicken, and cook for 10 to 12 minutes

SPICY

Add 1 tsp (5 mL) cayenne pepper

Cajun Crusty Calamari

INGREDIENTS

1 cup (250 mL) milk

2 lbs (900 g) squid, cleaned (include the tentacles, but don't slice – only slice the tubular body of the squid into half inch/1.25 cm rings)

Vegetable oil for deep frying

2 cups (500 mL) corn flakes

1 cup (250 mL) all-purpose flour

1 tsp (5 mL) cornstarch

1/2 tsp (2 mL) sea salt

1 tsp (5 mL) black pepper

1 tsp (5 mL) cayenne pepper

2 eggs

Lemon wedges for garnish

SERVES 4

METHOD

1. In a medium bowl, combine milk and squid. Allow to soak, covered and refrigerated, overnight or for at least 4 to 6 hours prior to frying.

2. Heat oil in an electric deep fryer set to 340°F (170°C).

3. In a blender, combine corn flakes, flour, cornstarch, salt, pepper and cayenne pepper. Pulse until mixture is blended fine. Transfer dry mixture to a bowl and set aside.

4. In another bowl, lightly beat eggs. Dip the squid into egg and then dredge in the crumb mixture, making sure all sides are well coated. Transfer battered squid to deep fryer basket and fry 4 to 5 minutes or until crispy and golden. Remove, drain on paper towel and serve with lemon wedges.

Although calamari originates from the Mediterranean-style of cooking, this fried squid recipe has a Louisiana-style batter that calls for corn flakes and cayenne pepper. Do note that you'll need to marinate the squid in milk some hours before frying; either 4 to 6 hours in advance or, if you wish, overnight.

CHANGE IT UP

VARIATION

For a non-crusty version, omit corn flakes and add 1 cup (250 mL) more all-purpose flour

SPICY

Add half tsp (2 mL) cayenne pepper to the dry mixture in step 3

Ken's Beer Batter Fish

INGREDIENTS

Vegetable oil for deep frying

$2\frac{1}{2}$ cups (625 mL) all-purpose flour

$\frac{1}{2}$ tsp (2 mL) sea salt

1 tsp (5 mL) white pepper

1 tbsp (15 mL) garlic powder

3 lbs (1350 g) haddock fillets, cut into half inch (1.25 cm) pieces

2 large eggs

1 cup (250 mL) milk

$\frac{1}{2}$ cup (175 mL) beer

SERVES 4 TO 6

METHOD

1. Heat oil in an electric deep fryer set to 340°F (170°C).

2. In a mixing bowl, combine flour, salt, pepper and garlic powder. Mix well. Dredge the fillets in the flour mixture and set aside on waxed paper.

3. Meanwhile, in a blender, combine eggs, milk and beer; blend until well mixed. Add remaining flour mixture and continue blending until batter is well combined.

4. Transfer batter to a bowl and dip flour-coated fillets in batter until both sides are well coated. Place fillets in deep fryer basket and fry 10 to 12 minutes or until golden brown. Drain on paper towel and serve.

Beer imparts a wonderful flavour to the haddock in this recipe. I tend to use stout or porter but the choice is yours. Serve these with chili fries, malt vinegar and tartar sauce.

CHANGE IT UP

VARIATIONS
Substitute 3 lbs large mushrooms or chicken for haddock

For a thinner batter, add half cup (125 mL) more milk

ADDITION
For an interesting twist, add 1 tsp (5 mL) cinnamon to flour mixture

SPICY
Add half tsp (2 mL) cayenne pepper to the batter

Chili Fries

INGREDIENTS

Vegetable oil for deep frying

3 large potatoes, cut into medium fries

4 tbsp (60 mL) chili powder

2 tbsp (30 mL) garlic powder

1 tsp (5 mL) sea salt

1 tsp (5 mL) black pepper

SERVES 4 TO 6

METHOD

1. Heat oil in an electric deep fryer set to 375°F (190°C).

2. Rinse the potato fries and pat dry with a paper towel. Set aside on wax paper.

3. Meanwhile, in a small bowl, combine chili powder, garlic powder, salt and pepper. Mix well.

4. Using a spoon, sprinkle fries with the dry mixture, making sure all are evenly coated.

5. Transfer coated fries to the deep fryer basket, filling to two-thirds only and being careful not to overcrowd the basket (you might have to fry in several batches). Fry 8 to 10 minutes or until crispy. Remove, drain on paper towel, and serve.

Chili-garlic fries are so good they could be eaten as a snack, accompanied only by ginger beer or shandy. Or take them on a picnic and serve with a cole slaw or a jicama, tomato and mint salad, topped with honey mustard dressing.

CHANGE IT UP

FOR GARLIC FRIES

Add 2 tbsp more garlic powder and, after frying, sprinkle fries with 2 tbsp (30 mL) of chopped, dried and roasted garlic

SPICY

Add 1 tbsp (15 mL) cayenne pepper to dry mixture

Sweet Potato Frites with Cinnamon

INGREDIENTS

Vegetable oil for deep frying

2 large sweet potatoes, peeled and sliced into very thin fries

1 tbsp (15 mL) all-purpose flour

2 tbsp (30 mL) ground cinnamon

1 tsp (5 mL) paprika

1/2 tsp (2 mL) sea salt

SERVES 4 TO 6

METHOD

1. Heat oil in an electric deep fryer set to 375°F (190°C).

2. Rinse the sweet potatoes and pat dry with a paper towel. Set aside on wax paper.

3. Meanwhile, in a small bowl, combine flour, cinnamon, paprika and salt. Mix well. Using a spoon, sprinkle sweet potato fries with the dry mixture, making sure fries are evenly coated.

4. Transfer coated fries to the deep fryer basket, filling to two-thirds only and being careful not to overcrowd the basket (you might have to fry in several batches). Fry 5 to 8 minutes or until crispy. Remove, drain on paper towel, and serve.

Sweet potato frites are so delicious – and sweet – it's surprising we don't eat these more often. Thin and elegant, these make an excellent side for sirloin steak or bouillabaisse.

CHANGE IT UP

SPICY
Add 1 tsp (5 mL) cayenne pepper to dry mixture

INDOOR GRILL

The Thrill of the Grill!

I love a barbecue and the taste of food seared on a grill. What I don't love is taking my life in my hands trying to light the thing. These are just a few of my favourite recipes. If you choose, you can prepare them on your outdoor barbecue with the bugs biting you and the flare-ups burning half the meat and leaving the rest raw…but why would you when the Inspire® Indoor Grill is so dependable and so convenient? The surface is non-stick, the heat is controllable, the excess fat and grease is captured in the drip tray for easy disposal, you can put the components in the dishwasher…and the taste is every bit as delicious as any gas barbecue you've ever owned. So it's up to you, but if you're going to be macho and venture into the great outdoors to cook – take a raincoat and don't forget the Deet.

Grilled Lamb with Lemon, Rosemary & Feta
Spicy-Grilled Scallops with Red Pepper Caviar
Portobello Mushrooms with Apple & Blue Cheese
Ken's Juicy Orange New York Steaks with Red Pepper
Mixed Seafood Grill with Lime & Mint
Grilled Lemon Chicken with Herbs
Pork Chops Grilled with Balsamic & Honey
Grilled Vegetables with Pineapple & Ginger
Grilled Maple Pears with Brown Sugar and Cinnamon

Oster

COUNTERTOP TO TABLE CUISINE

Grilled Lamb with Lemon, Rosemary & Feta

INGREDIENTS

1 small red onion, finely chopped

2 cloves garlic, chopped OR 1 tsp (5 mL) bottled minced garlic

1/4 cup (50 mL) balsamic vinegar

1/4 cup (50 mL) lemon juice

1/4 cup (50 mL) liquid honey

1/4 cup (50 mL) olive oil

2 tbsp (15 mL) dried rosemary OR 4 tbsp (30 mL) chopped fresh

1/2 tsp (2 mL) sea salt

1/2 tsp (2 mL) black pepper

8 lamb chops

1/2 cup (125 mL) crumbled feta cheese

SERVES 4

METHOD

1. In a blender or food processor, combine onion, garlic, balsamic vinegar, lemon, honey, oil, rosemary, salt and pepper. Set to pulse and/or chop until vegetables are finely chopped and mixture is well blended. Reserve 1/4 for basting in a covered bowl and refrigerate.

2. Transfer remaining blender mixture to a large bowl or large resealable freezer bag. Add lamb and marinate, covered in the refrigerator, overnight or for at least 4 to 8 hours before grilling.

3. Set indoor grill to 450°F (230°C) and spray surface with non-stick cooking oil. Grill lamb chops 4 to 5 minutes per side, basting occasionally with reserved mixture.

4. When ready, serve hot with crumbled feta on top.

To truly savour the lemon-rosemary-flavoured lamb, it's best to marinate the chops overnight. Serve with herbed mashed potatoes or tabbouleh and stuffed artichokes.

CHANGE IT UP

VARIATIONS

Substitute pork chops or beef steak for lamb

Substitute half cup (125 mL) goat cheese for feta cheese

ADDITION

Add quarter cup (50 mL) olive oil to make salad dressing

SPICY

Add 1 tsp (5 mL) hot sauce to step 1

Spicy-Grilled Scallops with Red Pepper Caviar

INGREDIENTS

1/2 tsp (2 mL) black pepper

1/2 tsp (2 mL) garlic powder

1/2 tsp (2 mL) sea salt

1/2 tsp (2 mL) cayenne pepper

1/2 tsp (2 mL) dried basil

1/2 tsp (2 mL) dried thyme

24 large scallops

RED PEPPER CAVIAR

2 sweet red peppers, seeded and finely chopped

1/2 small red onion, chopped

1 clove garlic, chopped

1/2 cup (125 mL) unsweetened apple juice

1/4 cup (50 mL) olive oil

1/4 cup (50 mL) balsamic vinegar

1/2 tsp (2 mL) dried basil

SERVES 4

METHOD

1. In a small bowl, combine pepper, garlic powder, salt, cayenne pepper, basil and thyme. Mix well. Add scallops and mix so that both sides are well coated. Set aside.

2. To prepare the red pepper caviar, and using a blender or food processor, finely chop the red peppers, onion and garlic. Add the apple juice, oil, balsamic vinegar and basil. Continue blending/chopping until well combined.

3. Set indoor grill to 450°F (230°C) and spray surface with non-stick cooking oil. Grill scallops 2 to 3 minutes per side.

4. Transfer 6 scallops to each plate, top with red pepper caviar and serve alongside salad or rice.

Don't let the "caviar" throw you: this version has nothing to do with fish eggs.

CHANGE IT UP

VARIATIONS

Substitute 24 large shrimp for scallops

Substitute 4 chicken breasts for scallops and grill 15 to 20 minutes, turning once

SPICY

Add half tsp (2 mL) hot sauce to the red pepper caviar.

Portobello Mushrooms with Apple & Blue Cheese

INGREDIENTS

4 large portobello mushrooms

DRESSING

$1/2$ cup (125 mL) crumbled blue cheese

$1/2$ cup (125 mL) plain yogurt

$1/4$ cup (50 mL) olive oil

2 tbsp (30 mL) white wine vinegar

$1/4$ cup (50 mL) applesauce

$1/4$ tsp (1 mL) dried basil

$1/4$ tsp (1 mL) dried thyme

MARINADE

$1/4$ cup (50 mL) balsamic vinegar

$1/4$ cup (50 mL) olive oil

$1/2$ tsp (2 mL) dried basil

$1/2$ tsp (2 mL) dried thyme

$1/2$ tsp (2 mL) sea salt

$1/2$ tsp (2 mL) black pepper

SERVES 4

METHOD

1. In a blender, combine blue cheese, yogurt, oil, vinegar, applesauce, basil and thyme. Blend until dressing is emulsified.

2. Meanwhile, in a medium bowl, combine balsamic vinegar, oil, basil, thyme, salt and pepper; mix well. Add mushrooms to bowl and allow to marinate for 30 minutes.

3. When mushrooms are ready, set indoor grill to 450°F (230°C) and grill mushrooms for 3 to 4 minutes, or until grill marks appear. Use some of the marinade to baste while grilling.

4. Top with blue cheese dressing and serve.

ENTERTAINING TIP

Use smaller portobello mushrooms and slice: serve as an appetizer

These mushrooms, topped with blue cheese, are perfect with mixed greens and herbed orzo topped with freshly grated Parmesan cheese.

CHANGE IT UP

VARIATION

Substitute 4 skinless, boneless chicken breasts for portobello mushrooms, and marinate for 2 to 4 hours prior to grilling. Grill 15 to 20 minutes.

Ken's Juicy Orange New York Steaks with Red Pepper

INGREDIENTS

1 small red onion, finely chopped

2 garlic cloves, chopped OR 1 tsp (5 mL) bottled minced garlic

1 small sweet red pepper, seeded and finely chopped

1 cup (250 mL) freshly squeezed orange juice with pulp

1/4 cup (50 mL) liquid honey

2 tbsp (30 mL) grated orange zest

1/2 tsp (2 mL) dried basil

1/2 tsp (2 mL) chili powder

1/2 tsp (2 mL) sea salt

1/2 tsp (2 mL) black pepper

2 1-lb New York steaks OR 2 top sirloin steaks

1 large seedless orange, peeled and sliced into half-inch circles, for garnish

My signature orange beef steaks are best when marinated longer. Prepare the marinade a day before serving and marinate steaks overnight in the refrigerator – you'll find the orange, honey, basil and chili completely permeate the steak with flavour. Serve this dish with penne in a marinara sauce or with grilled or pan-roasted vegetables.

SERVES 2

METHOD

1. In a blender or food processor, combine onion, garlic, pepper, orange juice, honey, zest, basil, chili powder, salt and pepper. Set to pulse and/or chop until vegetables are finely chopped and mixture is well blended. Reserve half for basting in a covered bowl and refrigerate.

2. Transfer remaining blender mixture to a large bowl or large, resealable freezer bag. Add steaks and marinate, covered in the refrigerator, overnight or for at least 6 to 8 hours prior to grilling.

3. Set indoor grill to 450°F (230°C) and spray surface with non-stick cooking spray. Grill steaks 5 to 6 minutes on each side, for rare, 7 to 8 minutes each side for medium, and 10 minutes for well done; baste throughout grilling time with reserve mixture. Last 5 minutes, grill the oranges on each side and use for garnish.

VEGETARIAN OPTION
Substitute 4 portobello mushrooms for beef but do not marinate: instead, use marinade only as a basting sauce while the mushrooms are grilling.

CHANGE IT UP

VARIATION
Replace beef with 2 chicken breasts, 10 to 12 extra-large shrimp or 2 large pork chops

Mixed Seafood Grill with Lime & Mint

INGREDIENTS

2 cloves garlic

1/4 cup (50 mL) lime juice

1 tsp (5 mL) grated lime zest

2 tbsp (30 mL) balsamic vinegar

1 tsp (5 mL) granulated sugar

1/2 tsp (2 mL) dried mint

1/2 tsp (2 mL) sea salt

1/2 tsp (2 mL) black pepper

4 8-inch bamboo skewers, soaked in water for 30 minutes before using

8 jumbo shrimp, peeled and deveined

1 8-oz (225 mL) swordfish steak, cut into 1 inch (2.5 cm) chunks

1 medium onion, cut into large pieces

1 large sweet red pepper, seeded and cut into large pieces

8 cherry tomatoes

SERVES 4

METHOD

1. In a mixing bowl, whisk together garlic, lime juice, zest, balsamic vinegar, sugar, mint, salt and pepper. Set basting mixture aside.

2. Thread shrimp, pepper, swordfish, onion and tomato, then repeat order, on each skewer. Baste kebabs with a brush or small spoon before grilling.

3. Set indoor grill to 450°F (230°C) and spray surface with a non-stick cooking oil. Grill seafood skewers, turning occasionally as you baste. Grill about 5 to 8 minutes or until shrimp is pink and swordfish opaque.

VEGETARIAN OPTION
Leave out the seafood and add zucchini, cauliflower and broccoli florets

ENTERTAINING TIP
Use shorter skewers and smaller shrimp and swordfish pieces

Serve these seafood kebabs on a bed of basmati rice, or on tart greens.

CHANGE IT UP

VARIATION
Replace the shrimp with large scallops

Grilled Lemon Chicken with Herbs

INGREDIENTS

1 cup (250 mL) white wine

1/4 cup (50 mL) lemon juice

2 cloves garlic, chopped OR 1 tsp (5 mL) bottled minced garlic

2 tbsp (30 mL) granulated sugar

1/2 tsp (2 mL) dried basil

1/2 tsp (2 mL) dried thyme

1/2 tsp (2 mL) dried oregano

1/2 tsp (2 mL) sea salt

1/2 tsp (2 mL) black pepper

4 skinless, boneless chicken breasts

This is a deliciously healthy chicken recipe I like to serve with a haricots verts salad tossed with a savoury vinaigrette or a pear and pecan salad with a balsamic Dijon vinaigrette.

SERVES 4

METHOD

1. In a medium bowl or large resealable freezer bag, combine wine, lemon juice, garlic, sugar, basil, thyme, oregano, salt and pepper. Reserve 1/4 of the mixture to use for basting and set aside. Add chicken, cover or seal, and marinate overnight or for at least 4 to 8 hours in refrigerator.

2. When fully marinated, grill chicken 20 to 25 minutes at 450°F (230°C), turning once half-way through and making sure the chicken has grill marks. Baste with reserve.

VEGETARIAN OPTION
Substitute 4 portobello mushrooms for chicken, and marinate for just 30 minutes

ENTERTAINING TIP
Slice chicken breasts and skewer with 2 cherry tomatoes per serving; grill 8 to 10 minutes. Should make about 18 to 20 skewers.

CHANGE IT UP

VARIATIONS
Substitute beef steak, pork or lamb for chicken and grill for 20 to 25 minutes

Substitute 15 to 18 jumbo shrimp for chicken

LOWER FAT OPTION
Replace sugar with equivalent low-calorie sweetener

Replace white wine with non-fat vegetable stock

Pork Chops Grilled with Balsamic & Honey

INGREDIENTS

¹/₄ cup (50 mL) balsamic vinegar

¹/₄ cup (50 mL) liquid honey

1 tbsp (15 mL) Dijon mustard

1 garlic clove, finely chopped OR ¹/₂ tsp (2 mL) bottled minced garlic

¹/₂ tsp (2 mL) dried basil

¹/₂ tsp (2 mL) sea salt

¹/₂ tsp (2 mL) black pepper

2 pork chops

SERVES 2

METHOD

1. In a medium mixing bowl, combine balsamic vinegar, honey, mustard, garlic, basil, salt and pepper. Whisk ingredients until well mixed. Set basting mixture aside.

2. Meanwhile, set indoor grill to 450°F (230°C) and spray surface with non-stick cooking oil. Once hot, quickly sear pork chops for 30 seconds each side, to create grill marks.

3. Once seared, return chops to grill and cook for about 8 to 10 minutes per side, depending on the thickness. Baste each side throughout the grilling process.

When grilled, these chops are brushed with a balsamic, honey mustard sauce that permeates these succulent chops. Serve with baked fennel or a warm spinach salad.

CHANGE IT UP

VARIATION

Substitute lamb chops or 2 firm fish fillets, such as swordfish or tuna, for pork chops

LOWER FAT OPTION

Substitute quarter cup (50 mL) orange juice for honey

Grilled Vegetables with Pineapple & Ginger

INGREDIENTS

PINEAPPLE DRESSING/MARINADE

2 tbsp (30 mL) olive oil

2 cloves garlic, chopped OR 1 tsp (5 mL) bottled minced garlic

1 small onion, finely chopped

$^3/_4$ cup (175 mL) pineapple juice

$^1/_4$ cup (50 mL) soy sauce

2 tbsp (30 mL) balsamic vinegar

2 tbsp (30 mL) sesame oil

1 tsp (5 mL) minced fresh ginger

$^1/_2$ tsp (2 mL) dried basil

$^1/_2$ tsp (2 mL) cayenne pepper

$^1/_2$ tsp (2 mL) sea salt

$^1/_2$ tsp (2 mL) black pepper

$^1/_2$ cup (125 mL) chopped pineapple

VEGETABLES

4 medium portobello mushrooms

1 medium sweet red pepper, seeded and quartered

1 medium green pepper, seeded and quartered

1 medium red onion, peeled and sliced 1-inch (2.5 cm) thick, or quartered

1 zucchini, cut into half-inch (1.25 cm) pieces

1 cup (250 mL) peeled baby carrots

1 cup (250 mL) broccoli florets

SERVES 4 TO 6

METHOD

1. In a blender, combine oil, garlic, onion, pineapple juice, soy sauce, balsamic vinegar, sesame oil, ginger, basil, cayenne pepper, salt and pepper. Blend until puréed.

2. Remove half the mixture, add pineapple pieces, and reserve for dressing; set aside. Transfer remaining blender mixture to a large bowl. Add mushrooms, peppers, onion, zucchini, carrots and broccoli and marinate for at least 30 minutes prior to grilling.

3. Set indoor grill to 450°F (230°C) and grill marinated vegetables for 6 to 8 minutes, occasionally basting with reserve dressing.

4. Once done, transfer grilled vegetables to a large salad bowl and add remaining pineapple dressing. Toss and serve.

This fusion of Asian (ginger, soy sauce, sesame oil) and "new world" flavours such as pineapple (which originates from south and central America) makes for an aromatic grill. An excellent accompaniment is a mixed grain pilaf, or raisin-studded quinoa or fragrant rice.

CHANGE IT UP

VARIATION

Substitute orange juice for pineapple juice and chopped orange for chopped pineapple

ADDITION

Add 14 to 16 medium shrimp; marinate and grill with vegetables

Maple Grilled Pears with Brown Sugar & Cinnamon

INGREDIENTS

4 large pears, cored, peeled and cut into 8 slices each

$1/4$ cup (50 mL) lemon juice

$1/2$ cup (125 mL) brown sugar

$1/2$ tbsp (10 mL) ground cinnamon

$1/2$ cup (125 mL) pure maple syrup

SERVES 4 TO 6

METHOD

1. In a large bowl, spoon lemon juice over pears.

2. In another bowl, combine brown sugar and cinnamon. Mix well.

3. Sprinkle brown sugar-cinnamon mixture over fleshy part of the pear slices so that each is well coated. Set indoor grill on high, add pear slices, and grill 4 to 5 minutes or until golden.

4. To serve, evenly distribute pear slices on 4 serving plates and drizzle with maple syrup.

These sugar-cinnamon-coated grilled pears are excellent served with ice cream or topped with yogurt. I sometimes drizzle with dark rum as well as maple syrup.

CHANGE IT UP

VARIATION

Substitute 4 peeled, cored and sliced apples or 4 peeled and sliced bananas/plantains for pears

LOWER FAT OPTION

Use calorie-reduced maple syrup

Use calorie-reduced sweetener instead of brown sugar

IN2ITIVE®
BLENDER/
FOOD PROCESSOR

Show it all!

Yes, it's time to get that blender out of the cupboard and put it right out there on the kitchen counter where it belongs. It's not just for special occasions or special dishes. This is a versatile appliance that can save you time and help you create some wonderful dishes every day of the year. The few recipes we've included here are just the beginning. Health drinks, baby foods, sauces, salsa, soups, purées and so much more can bring variety and excitement to your meal times. Once you try these recipes you'll be hooked and that blender will never go back in the cupboard again.

Espresso Oreo™ Ice Cream Delight
Creamy Eggs & Ham with Parmesan
Three-Mushroom Soup with White Wine
Easy Crabmeat Bisque with Red Wine & Thyme
Creamy Broccoli & Cauliflower Soup with Blue Cheese
Sun-Dried Tomato Salsa with Fresh Parsley & Lime
Sweet Onion Relish with Red Pepper & Espresso
Coriander Citrus Marinade with Honey & Garlic

Dessert in a Blender
Espresso Oreo™ Ice Cream Delight

INGREDIENTS

6 Oreo™ cookies

$1/2$ cup (125 mL) espresso

1 banana, peeled and coarsely chopped

$1/2$ cup (125 mL) chocolate sauce

2 cups (500 mL) vanilla ice cream

1 tbsp (15 mL) chopped fresh mint

Sprig of mint leaves for garnish

SERVES 2 TO 4

METHOD

1. In a blender, combine cookies, espresso, banana, chocolate sauce, ice cream and mint. Blend until smooth.

2. Transfer mixture to medium bowl. Cover and place in the freezer for about half an hour prior to serving.

3. When ready to serve, spoon into 2 to 4 bowls and garnish with fresh mint.

This "dessert in a blender" is fabulously quick and easy to make, and absolutely scrumptious.

CHANGE IT UP

VARIATION
Replace Oreo™ cookies with 6 peanut butter cookies or $1/2$ cup (125 mL) crunchy peanut butter

ADDITION
Add 2 oz (56 mL) Kahlua coffee liqueur to blender

Breakfast in a Blender
Creamy Eggs & Ham with Parmesan

INGREDIENTS

4 thick slices cooked ham, coarsely chopped

1 small red onion, peeled and coarsely chopped

1 small sweet red pepper, seeded and coarsely chopped

1 small tomato, coarsely chopped

4 large eggs

$1/4$ cup (50 mL) table cream

$1/4$ cup (50 mL) Parmesan cheese

$1/2$ tsp (2 mL) chili powder

$1/2$ tsp (2 mL) sea salt

$1/2$ tsp (2 mL) black pepper

SERVES 2 TO 4

METHOD

1. In a blender, combine ham, onion, pepper, tomato, eggs, cream, Parmesan, chili powder, salt and pepper. Set to pulse or "salsa" setting and blend well.

2. In a non-stick skillet on 450°F (230°C) scramble the egg mixture about 4 to 5 minutes or until cooked.

COOKING OPTION

To bake instead of scrambling, set toaster oven to 350°F (175°C). Place mixture into a non-stick cake pan, about 7" x 4" x 2", and bake 15 to 18 minutes, mixing with a fork once. Make toast in the last 5 minutes and serve with eggs.

This "breakfast in a blender" is like an omelet, but especially fluffy. Serve this with salsa on the side or with a heaping dollop of yogurt or sour cream.

CHANGE IT UP

VARIATION

Replace ham with 6 slices cooked bacon, chopped, or 4 cooked breakfast sausages, chopped

LOWER FAT OPTION

Use 2 eggs and half cup (175 mL) egg whites

Use lean, low-fat cooked ham

Use light Parmesan cheese

Use skim milk instead of cream

SPICY

Add half tsp (2 mL) cayenne pepper to the mixture

Soup in a Blender
Three-Mushroom Soup with White Wine

INGREDIENTS

2 cups (500 mL) chopped button mushrooms

1 cup (250 mL) chopped shiitake mushrooms

2 portobello mushrooms, chopped

1 small red onion, chopped

2 cloves garlic, chopped OR 1 tsp (5 mL) bottled minced garlic

1 small sweet red pepper, seeded and chopped

1 tbsp (15 mL) Dijon mustard

1/2 tsp (2 mL) dried basil

1/2 tsp (2 mL) dried oregano

1/2 tsp (2 mL) sea salt

1/2 tsp (2 mL) black pepper

4 cups (1 L) vegetable stock

1/2 cup (125 mL) white wine

1 cup (250 mL) table cream

The best mushroom soup is homemade; but even better than homemade is mushroom soup made with portobellos and shiitakes and flavoured with cream, Dijon mustard and white wine.

SERVES 4 TO 6

METHOD

1. In a blender, combine mushrooms, onion, garlic, pepper, mustard, basil, oregano, salt and pepper. Set to pulse or "soup" setting until vegetables are finely chopped and well mixed.

2. In a rice cooker, add vegetable stock and white wine. Transfer blender mixture to rice cooker, cover, and allow to boil until warm light illuminates.

3. Remove lid and add cream; mix well and serve.

ENTERTAINING TIP
To create mushroom bruschetta, transfer blended mixture to a skillet with 2 tbsp (15 mL) olive oil and cook for 8 to 10 minutes. Spoon cooked mixture onto crusted bread, brushed with olive oil and rubbed with garlic. Place into toaster oven and broil for a few minutes before serving.

CHANGE IT UP

VARIATIONS

To make pasta sauce: Use blended mixture sautéed in a skillet with half cup (125 mL) cream for 8 to 10 minutes

For a smoother texture, use a hand blender and purée soup while still in the rice cooker

For a richer flavour, substitute whipping cream for table cream

Substitute portobello or shiitake mushrooms with cremini mushrooms, or any type you prefer

LOWER FAT OPTION

Use low-fat/non-fat vegetable stock

Substitute skim milk for table cream

Soup in a Blender
Easy Crabmeat Bisque with Red Wine & Thyme

INGREDIENTS

1 19-oz (540 mL) can stewed and diced tomatoes

4 cups (1 L) vegetable stock

1/2 cup (125 mL) red wine

1/2 cup (125 mL) mild salsa

2 tbsp (30 mL) liquid honey

1 tsp (5 mL) dried thyme

1/2 tsp (2 mL) sea salt

1/2 tsp (2 mL) black pepper

2 cloves garlic, chopped OR 1/2 tsp (2 mL) bottled minced garlic

1 small sweet red pepper, seeded and coarsely chopped

1 small red onion, peeled and chopped

2 cups (500 mL) crabmeat

1 cup (250 mL) table cream

SERVES 4 TO 6

METHOD

1. In a rice cooker, add tomatoes, vegetable stock, red wine, salsa, honey, thyme, sea salt and pepper. Allow to boil until "warm" light illuminates.

2. Meanwhile, in a blender, combine garlic, red pepper, onion and crabmeat. Set to pulse or "soup" setting and blend until vegetables and crabmeat are finely chopped and well mixed.

3. Transfer blender mixture to rice cooker and reset. Cook until warm light illuminates.

4. While soup is still in rice cooker, add cream. Using a hand blender, purée until soup is smooth.

Bisque is a marvelously rich soup usually made with cream and puréed seafood. This version calls for crabmeat, but the addition of red wine, salsa, honey and thyme makes this a particularly yummy and bodacious bisque.

CHANGE IT UP

VARIATION
Replace the crabmeat with equivalent amount of shrimp or lobster

ADDITION
For a richer flavour use only half cup (125 mL) table cream and add half cup (125 mL) whipping cream

LOWER FAT OPTION
Substitute skim milk for cream

SPICY
Add 1 jalapeno pepper, seeded and chopped, to blender

Creamy Broccoli & Cauliflower Soup with Blue Cheese

INGREDIENTS

5 cups (1.25 L) vegetable stock

3 cloves garlic, chopped OR 1½ tsp (7 mL) bottled minced garlic

1 small red onion, peeled and coarsely chopped

2 cups (500 mL) chopped broccoli florets

2 cups (500 mL) chopped cauliflower florets

1 small green pepper, seeded and coarsely chopped

1 cup (250 mL) table cream

½ cup (125 mL) crumbled blue cheese

½ tsp (2 mL) sea salt

½ tsp (2 mL) black pepper

SERVES 4 TO 6

METHOD

1. In a saucepot or rice cooker, add soup stock. Cover and bring to a boil.

2. Meanwhile, in a blender, combine garlic, onion, broccoli, cauliflower and green pepper. Set to pulse or "soup" setting until vegetables are finely chopped and well mixed.

3. Add to rice cooker and cook until warm light illuminates.

4. Remove lid and add cream, blue cheese, salt and pepper. Stir until smooth and serve.

Broccoli and cauliflower combined with blue cheese and cream makes for one of my favourite soups. Whenever I serve this to friends, they can't get enough and beg for the recipe. Serve this with melted-brie toasts on the side.

CHANGE IT UP

VARIATION
Substitute gorgonzola for the blue cheese

ADDITION
For extra-rich flavour, use only half cup (125 mL) table cream and add half cup (125 mL) whipping cream

LOWER FAT OPTION
Omit table cream and replace with 1 cup (250 mL) skim milk

COUNTERTOP TO TABLE CUISINE

Sun-Dried Tomato Salsa with Fresh Parsley & Lime

INGREDIENTS

2 celery stalks, chopped

1 small red onion, coarsely chopped

1 cup (250 mL) coarsely chopped sun-dried tomatoes

2 medium tomatoes, coarsely chopped

2 cloves garlic, chopped OR 1 tsp (5 mL) bottled minced garlic

1/2 cup (125 mL) chopped fresh parsley

3/4 cup (175 mL) tomato juice

2 tbsp (30 mL) olive oil

2 tbsp (30 mL) lime juice

2 tbsp (30 mL) liquid honey

2 tbsp (30 mL) balsamic vinegar

1 tsp (5 mL) chili powder

1/2 tsp (2 mL) sea salt

1 tsp (5 mL) black pepper

1/2 cup (125 mL) corn kernels, canned or frozen and thawed

MAKES 3 cups

METHOD

1. In a blender, combine celery, onion, sun-dried tomatoes, tomatoes, garlic, parsley, tomato juice, honey, balsamic vinegar, chili powder, salt and pepper. Set to pulse or "salsa" setting. If necessary, pulse twice to ensure mixture is chopped fine.

2. Transfer mixture to a medium bowl, add corn and mix well.

3. Refrigerate, covered, at least 2 hours prior to serving.

ENTERTAINING TIP

To make bruschetta: Set oven to broil. Meanwhile, thinly slice a loaf of bread, rubbing one side with a peeled and halved clove of garlic. Brush garlic-rubbed side with olive oil. Arrange bread on baking sheet, garlic-side up. Spoon relish on to each bread slice and place in oven. Broil for 1 to 2 minutes or until bread is slightly toasted.

This sweet-spicy, citrus-y salsa is perfect for serving alongside omelets or frittatas.

CHANGE IT UP

VARIATION

Substitute coriander for chopped fresh flat-leaf (Italian) parsley

ADDITION

In a saucepot, heat and serve as a pasta sauce, or add 2 cups (500 mL) cooked red kidney beans for vegetarian chili

Sweet Onion Relish with Red Pepper & Espresso

INGREDIENTS

4 small red onions, peeled and coarsely chopped

1 small sweet red pepper, seeded and coarsely chopped

2 cups (500 mL) vegetable stock

1/2 cup (125 mL) espresso

1/2 cup (125 mL) liquid honey

2 tbsp (30 mL) balsamic vinegar

1/2 tsp (2 mL) dried basil

1/2 tsp (2 mL) dried thyme

1/2 tsp (2 mL) sea salt

1/2 tsp (2 mL) black pepper

MAKES 3 TO 4 cups

METHOD

1. In a blender, combine onions, pepper, vegetable stock, espresso, honey, balsamic vinegar, basil, thyme, salt and pepper. Set to pulse or "salsa" setting until vegetables are finely chopped and well mixed.

2. Transfer relish to an electric skillet set to 450°F (230°C). Simmer for about 8 to 10 minutes or until the relish has been reduced by half.

3. Transfer to a bowl and serve warm or cold.

This divinely sweet relish is spiked with espresso and is a tasty accompaniment for hamburgers, chicken, pork, fish, shellfish or vegetables.

CHANGE IT UP

VARIATIONS

Reserve 1 cup (250 mL) and use as a base for soups or stews

To make a salad dressing: Reserve half cup (125 mL) and add quarter cup (50 mL) olive oil and 2 tbsp (30 mL) wine vinegar

To make a sauce: Reserve half cup (125 mL) and add half cup (125 mL) table cream. Simmer in a skillet on medium for 10 minutes

SPICY

Add 1 tsp (5 mL) hot sauce to blender

Coriander Citrus Marinade with Honey & Garlic

INGREDIENTS

2 cups (500 mL) freshly squeezed orange juice

1 seedless orange, peeled and coarsely chopped

1 small red onion, peeled and coarsely chopped

4 cloves garlic, chopped OR 2 tsp (10 mL) bottled minced garlic

1/2 cup (125 mL) olive oil

1/2 cup (125 mL) liquid honey

2 tbsp (30 mL) grated orange zest

2 tbsp (30 mL) lime juice

1/2 cup (125 mL) chopped fresh coriander

1/2 tsp (2 mL) sea salt

1/2 tsp (2 mL) black pepper

MAKES 3 cups

METHOD

1. In a blender, combine orange juice, orange, onion, garlic, oil, honey, zest, lime juice, coriander, salt and pepper. Set to pulse and blend until just diced.

2. Transfer to a large bowl, cover and refrigerate. Use in the next 2 or 3 days by marinating seafood, chicken, beef, pork or vegetables overnight or for 4 to 6 hours minimum before cooking.

I make this marinade whenever I'm grilling meat for a Thai-themed meal. Try this as a marinade for grilled and skewered jumbo shrimp, served over a bed of fragrant rice and accompanied by green mango salad and coconut chicken soup.

CHANGE IT UP

VARIATIONS

To make a citrus salad dressing: Reserve quarter cup (50 mL) and add quarter (50 mL) olive oil and 2 tbsp (30 mL) wine vinegar

To make a sauce: Reserve quarter cup (50 mL) and add half cup (125 mL) cream. In a saucepan, on medium heat, stir for about 10 minutes and reduce by half

For soup: Reserve 1 cup (250 mL) and use as a soup stock base for chicken or seafood

BLENDER

To your good health!

You're tired and run down. You need something refreshing
so you reach for your blender! In minutes you can mix a
delicious, healthy, nutritious drink that will build your energy
level and help power you through the day. Keep your
versatile blender on the kitchen counter and a supply of
fresh fruits and vegetables on hand. Try these invigorating
recipes instead of a can of pop. Be inventive with your
ingredients and, if you add in a little of your favourite spirit
at the end of the day...enjoy.

Caramel Heaven with Pineapple Shake
Raspberry Deluxe Lassi
Orange Soy Mint Shake
Tropical Love Shake
Berry, Berry Good Lassi
Green to the Core Shake
Wake Up Little Smoothie

Caramel Heaven Pineapple Shake

INGREDIENTS

1 cup (250 mL) pineapple juice

1 cup (250 mL) orange juice

1/2 cup (125 mL) caramel sauce

1/2 cup (125 mL) pineapple chunks

1/2 tsp (2 mL) vanilla extract

1 cup (250 mL) vanilla ice cream

Pineapple slices for garnish (optional)

SERVES 3 TO 4

METHOD

1. In a blender, combine juices, caramel sauce, pineapple, vanilla extract and ice cream. Blend until smooth.

2. Serve in chilled glasses, garnish with pineapple slices (if using), and serve.

This is truly a heavenly tropical treat; serve in place of dessert on a hot summer night.

CHANGE IT UP

VARIATION

To make a frozen yogurt shake, replace ice cream with 1 cup (250 mL) yogurt and add 1 cup (250 mL) ice

ADDITION

Add 2 to 3 oz (56 to 84 mL) dark rum to blender and serve in chilled cocktail glasses

Raspberry Deluxe Lassi

INGREDIENTS

1 cup (250 mL) cranberry juice

1 cup (250 mL) raspberry juice

2 tbsp (30 mL) lemon juice

2 cups (500 mL) fresh raspberries

2 tbsp (30 mL) raspberry jam

1/2 cup (125 mL) raspberry yogurt

2 tbsp (30 mL) liquid honey

Raspberries and sliced strawberries (optional)

SERVES 2 TO 3

METHOD

1. In a blender, combine juices, raspberries, jam, yogurt and honey. Blend until smooth and foamy.

2. Pour into chilled glasses, garnish with berries (if using), and serve.

A lassi is a popular Southeast Asian drink traditionally made with plain yogurt, honey and spices and served after a meal. My version is ripe with fresh strawberries, strawberry yogurt and other fruit juices. Serve for breakfast or as part of your brunch.

CHANGE IT UP

VARIATION
Replace yogurt with raspberry ice cream

ADDITION
Add 2 to 3 oz (56 to 84 mL) vodka or light rum

Orange Soy Mint Shake

INGREDIENTS

1 cup (250 mL) chilled soy milk

2 tbsp (30 mL) grated orange zest

2 seedless oranges, peeled and quartered

1 cup (250 mL) freshly squeezed orange juice

2 tbsp (30 mL) chopped fresh mint

1 cup (250 mL) ice

1 sprig fresh mint (optional)

SERVES 2 TO 3

METHOD

1. In a blender, combine soy milk, zest, oranges, juice, mint and ice. Blend until smooth.

2. Pour into chilled glasses, garnish with fresh mint (if using), and serve.

This has got be one of the most delicious and refreshing shakes going, particularly if you like the nutty flavour of soy. If you want to add a little bit of heft, add half cup coarsely chopped medium-firm tofu to blender: this will make it even creamier.

CHANGE IT UP

ADDITIONS

Add 1 cup (500 mL) orange sherbet

Add 2 to 3 oz (56 to 84 mL) Grand Marnier liqueur

Tropical Love Shake

INGREDIENTS

$^1/_2$ cup (125 mL) coconut milk

1 cup (250 mL) freshly squeezed orange juice

1 cup (250 mL) pineapple juice

$^1/_2$ cup (125 mL) pineapple pieces

1 small banana, peeled and coarsely chopped

1 cup (250 mL) papaya peeled, seeded and chopped

$^1/_4$ cup (50 mL) flaked, unsweetened coconut

$^1/_2$ cup (125 mL) vanilla ice cream

1 cup (250 mL) ice

Pineapple slices for garnish (optional)

SERVES 2 TO 3

METHOD

1. In a blender, combine milk, juices, pineapple, banana, papaya, coconut, ice cream and ice. Blend until smooth and foamy.

2. Pour into chilled glasses, garnish with pineapple slices (if using), and serve.

If you love the tropics, you'll love this piece of paradise. It calls for coconut, papaya, banana, orange and pineapple. (If using canned, instead of fresh pineapple, drain first before adding to the blender.)

CHANGE IT UP

ADDITION

Add 2 to 3 oz (56 to 84 mL) coconut liqueur or rum and serve in chilled martini or cocktail glasses

Berry, Berry Good Lassi

INGREDIENTS

1/2 cup (125 mL) unsweetened raspberry juice

1 cup (250 mL) unsweetened cranberry juice

1 cup (250 mL) unsweetened blueberry juice

1/2 cup (125 mL) strawberries, fresh or frozen and thawed

1/2 cup (125 mL) raspberries, fresh or frozen and thawed

1/2 cup (125 mL) blueberries, fresh or frozen and thawed

1/2 cup (125 mL) plain yogurt

2 tbsp (30 mL) liquid honey

1 cup (250 mL) ice

Berries for garnish (optional)

SERVES 2 TO 3

METHOD

1. In a blender, combine juices, strawberries, raspberries, blueberries, yogurt, honey and ice. Blend until smooth.

2. Pour into chilled glasses, garnish with raspberries, blueberries and sliced strawberries (if using), and serve.

This is a refreshing yogurt-and-honey drink, that you'll find berry, berry good!

CHANGE IT UP

ADDITION
Add 2 oz (56 mL) vodka to the blender for a bit of a Cossack kick; serve in chilled martini glasses

Green to the Core Shake

INGREDIENTS

1 cup (250 mL) green tea

1 cup (250 mL) unsweetened apple juice

1/2 cup (125 mL) canned or fresh kiwi juice

2 kiwi, peeled and quartered

1/2 cup (125 mL) honeydew melon

1 small green apple, peeled, cored and quartered

2 tbsp (30 mL) liquid honey

2 tbsp (30 mL) chopped fresh mint

1 cup (250 mL) ice

1 sprig of fresh mint (optional)

SERVES 2 TO 3

METHOD

1. In a blender, combine green tea, juices, kiwi, melon, apple, honey, mint and ice. Blend until smooth.

2. Pour into chilled glasses, garnish with fresh mint (if using), and serve.

Green tea has been shown to boost the immune system and reduce cholesterol and arteriosclerosis. Complemented by apples, kiwi, melon, honey and fresh mint, this packs one powerhouse punch.

CHANGE IT UP

VARIATION
Add 1 cup (250 mL) lime sherbet to the blender for a creamier shake

ADDITION
Add 2 to 3 oz (56 to 84 mL) Crème de Menthe liqueur to the blender and serve in chilled martini glasses, garnished with fresh mint

Wake Up Little Smoothie

INGREDIENTS

1 cup (250 mL) freshly squeezed orange juice

1 cup (250 mL) unsweetened apple juice

1 small seedless orange, peeled and chopped

1 small apple, peeled, cored and chopped

1 small banana, peeled and chopped

1/2 cup (125 mL) plain yogurt

2 tbsp (30 mL) liquid honey

1/2 cup (125 mL) ice

Orange slices, for garnish

SERVES 2 TO 3

METHOD

1. In a blender, combine juices, orange, apple, banana, yogurt, honey and ice. Set to "smoothie" setting and blend for 30 to 45 seconds.

2. Transfer to chilled glasses, garnish with orange slices, and serve.

As the name suggests, this is a perfect morning treat: it's sweet, light and nourishing.

CHANGE IT UP

VARIATION
Substitute 1 pear, peeled, cored and chopped for the apple, and replace the apple juice with 1 cup pear nectar

ADDITION
Add 2 to 3 oz (56 to 84 mL) of light or dark rum to the blender and serve – later in the day – in chilled martini glasses garnished with a thin apple or pear slice

COUNTERTOP TO TABLE CUISINE

COFFEEMAKER/ COFFEE BURR MILL

My Cup Runneth Over

I admit it. I am addicted to coffee, and I've found so many ways to enjoy it. Try these delicious recipes and you'll be hooked too. But it's important to start with good coffee. Choose your favourite beans and grind them fresh in a coffee mill. Use cold, clear water and brew it strong enough to bring out the full rich flavour, and use it while it's fresh and at the peak of flavour. All the coffee used to test these recipes was prepared with the Oster® 12-Cup Programmable Coffeemaker. That way I could 'Pause 'n Serve' to enjoy a cup while I was cooking, and I could adjust the strength to meet the needs of the various recipes. Coffee is one of the most distinctive and comforting flavours in the universe. Try these recipes and enjoy the taste of coffee all day long.

Espresso Shortbread with Cinnamon
Espresso Biscotti with Raisins
Espresso Peanut Butter Cookies
Coffee Ice Cream with Cookies
Coffee Hot Chocolate with Marshmallows
Coffee-Glazed Turkey with Strawberries

Espresso Shortbread with Cinnamon

INGREDIENTS

1 cup (250 mL) unsalted butter, softened

1/2 cup (125 mL) icing sugar

2 cups (500 mL) sifted all-purpose flour

1/4 cup (50 mL) espresso OR strong coffee

1 tsp (5 mL) vanilla extract

1 tsp (5 mL) ground cinnamon

MAKES **30** small cookies

METHOD

1. In a food processor, combine butter and icing sugar, and process until smooth and fluffy. Add flour, espresso, vanilla and cinnamon, and continue processing until mixture has a doughy consistency.

2. Line a toaster oven pan with parchment paper. Using a teaspoonful of batter for each cookie, form a ball with your hands and place on lined oven pan. Using your thumb, press a small dimple in the middle.

3. Bake in toaster oven at 350°F (175°C) for 10 to 12 minutes or until edges are lightly browned.

At one time these butter-rich cookies were only enjoyed during festive seasons, but not anymore. Another break with tradition is the adding of espresso to the batter. For a little flourish, just before baking press a chocolate-covered coffee bean into the top center.

CHANGE IT UP

ADDITION
Add nuts or mixed fruit such as raisins, dates, dried apricots, craisins or cherries to the cookies

LOWER FAT OPTION
For a harder, much-less rich and lower-fat shortbread cookie, substitute margarine for butter

Espresso Biscotti with Raisins

INGREDIENTS

$1/2$ cup (125 mL) unsalted butter, softened

1 cup (250 mL) granulated sugar

1 large egg

$1/4$ cup (50 mL) espresso OR strong coffee

1 tsp (5 mL) vanilla extract

2 cups (500 mL) sifted all-purpose flour

1 tsp (5 mL) baking powder

A pinch of salt

$1/2$ cup (125 mL) raisins

These biscotti are delicious dipped in coffee or broken up and mixed in with yogurt or ice cream.

MAKES approximately 25 biscotti

METHOD

1. In a food processor, combine butter and sugar and process until light and fluffy. Add egg and mix well. Continue processing and add vanilla extract and espresso. Add the flour, baking powder, salt and raisins and process until well mixed.

2. Meanwhile, line toaster oven pan with parchment paper. Remove biscotti batter from food processor and, using your hands, roll dough into 2 logs, the length of the pan and roughly 2 inches in diameter.

3. Place biscotti logs on parchment-lined pan and transfer to toaster oven. Bake on top level at 350°F (175°C) for 25 minutes or until golden brown. remove and cool.Remove and let cool for 10 minutes.

4. Place logs on cutting board and, using a serrated knife, slice each log diagonally at a 45-degree angle into half inch pieces. Lay flat on baking pan and return to toaster oven. Bake for 5 minutes, turn over, and bake for another 5 minutes more or until slightly dried and golden brown all over.

CHANGE IT UP

VARIATION

Replace raisins with a combination of nuts or dried cranberries

Espresso Peanut Butter Cookies

INGREDIENTS

1 cup (250 mL) unsalted butter, softened

1¼ cups (300 mL) smooth peanut butter

1 cup (250 mL) granulated sugar

1 cup (250 mL) brown sugar

½ cup (125 mL) espresso OR strong coffee

2 large eggs

2 tsp (10 mL) vanilla extract

3 cups (750 mL) sifted all-purpose flour

2 tsp (10 mL) baking soda

MAKES approximately 25 cookies

METHOD

1. In a blender, combine butter and peanut butter and process until smooth and fluffy. Add granulated and brown sugar and mix. Next add coffee, eggs and vanilla extract, and continue processing. Add flour and baking soda until mixture has doughy consistency.

2. Using a tablespoonful of batter for each cookie, form a ball with your hands and place on a parchment paper-lined toaster oven pan. Press each cookie ball with a fork to flatten slightly.

3. Bake in the toaster oven at 375°F (190°C) for 15 minutes or until lightly browned.

Like that classic pairing of chocolate and peanut butter, espresso and peanut butter makes for a scrumptious match.

CHANGE IT UP

VARIATION

For a more textured cookie, substitute crunchy peanut butter

LOWER FAT OPTION

Use margarine and a calorie-reduced peanut butter

Coffee Ice Cream with Cookies

INGREDIENTS

1 cup (250 mL) strong coffee OR espresso

6 chocolate chip cookies, broken into pieces

1 banana, peeled and coarsely chopped

1 cup (250 mL) whole milk

1 cup (250 mL) coffee ice cream

1/4 cup (50 mL) chocolate sauce

1/4 tsp (1 mL) cinnamon

1/4 tsp (1 mL) nutmeg

SERVES 4

METHOD

1. In a blender, combine espresso, cookies, banana, milk, ice cream, chocolate sauce, cinnamon and nutmeg. If using an In2itive® blender, use milkshake setting. If using another blender, blend until frothy but chunky and semi-smooth.

2. Apportion into 4 cups or bowls and serve with a straw as a beverage or with a spoon as a dessert.

This delicious, frothy treat can be served as a dessert or an ice cream shake. If you do serve in dessert bowls, garnish with crumbled chocolate chip cookies.

CHANGE IT UP

LOWER FAT OPTION

Substitute skim milk or non-fat milk for whole milk

Substitute low-fat ice cream for ice cream

Substitute low-fat cookies for chocolate chip cookies

Omit the chocolate sauce

Coffee Hot Chocolate with Marshmallows

2 cups (500 mL) very hot whole milk

1 cup (250 mL) hot coffee

2 tbsp (30 mL) unsweetened cocoa powder

2 tbsp (30 mL) brown sugar OR $1/4$ cup (50 mL) liquid honey

1 oz (28 mL) semi-sweet chocolate

$1/2$ tsp (2 mL) vanilla extract

1 cup (250 mL) small marshmallows

MAKES 2 TO 3 cups

METHOD

1. In a blender, combine milk, coffee, cocoa powder, brown sugar, chocolate and vanilla. Blend until smooth.

2. Transfer coffee-chocolate drink to cups. Top with marshmallows and serve hot.

This hot chocolate, spiked with coffee and mellowed with marshmallows, is perfect for pre or après ski. Serve with apple fritters and profiteroles (cream puffs).

CHANGE IT UP

LOWER FAT OPTION

Substitute skim milk for whole milk

Coffee-Glazed Turkey with Strawberries

INGREDIENTS

3/4 cup (175 mL) strong coffee

2 cloves garlic, chopped OR 1/2 tsp (2 mL) bottled minced garlic

1 cup (250 mL) molasses

3/4 cup (175 mL) strawberry jam

1/2 cup (125 mL) fresh strawberries

2 tbsp (30 mL) balsamic vinegar

1 tbsp (15 mL) Dijon mustard

1 tsp (5 mL) vanilla extract

1 skinless, boneless turkey breast, sliced in half

SERVES 2 TO 4

METHOD

1. In a blender or food processor, combine coffee, garlic, molasses, jam, strawberries, balsamic vinegar, Dijon mustard and vanilla extract. Blend or process until smooth. Reserve half the coffee mixture and set aside.

2. Preheat oven or toaster oven to 375°F (190°C). Meanwhile, transfer turkey into a greased or foil-lined oven pan and pour coffee mixture over turkey.

3. Place pan in oven or toaster oven and bake for 30 to 35 minutes, occasionally basting with reserved coffee mixture.

Cooking, marinating, or glazing with coffee, honey and fruit livens up any meat or fowl. Serve these sliced turkey breasts on a bed of greens or wild rice pilaf and garnish with sliced strawberries soaked in balsamic vinegar.

CHANGE IT UP

VARIATIONS

Use 2 skinless, boneless chicken breasts instead of turkey, but bake for only 20 to 25 minutes

Substitute beef roast for turkey

TOASTER OVEN

And you can use it for toasting bread too!

Just look at these recipes. Swordfish, lamb chops, chicken, burgers, biscuits...all cooked to perfection without turning on your oven. The Inspire® Toaster Oven has double wall construction so it keeps all the heat inside where it belongs, and that keeps your kitchen cool. It's easy to regulate the heat. Easy to set the time. Easy to clean. And once you try these recipes you'll see that a toaster oven can do everything a big oven can do...in less time and using less energy. As for toast...well, here's to your Inspire® Toaster Oven!

Pork Tenderloin with a Pear & Blue Cheese Sauce
Bacon-Wrapped Scallops with Grapefruit, Dill & Vodka
Swordfish Steaks with Dijon & Tarragon
Cajun Burgers with Red Pepper & Parmesan
Curry Lamb Chops with Mint
Almond Biscotti with Cinnamon & Maple Syrup
Sesame Honey Garlic Chicken with Salsa
Orange Garlic Basil Shrimp
Roasted Vegetables with Dijon, Rosemary & Balsamic
Ken's Orange Biscuits

Pork Tenderloin with a Pear & Blue Cheese Sauce

INGREDIENTS

2 pears, peeled, cored and chopped

1 small red onion, coarsely chopped

1/2 tsp (2 mL) dried basil OR 2 tbsp (30 mL) chopped fresh

1/2 tsp (2 mL) dried thyme OR 2 tbsp (30 mL) chopped fresh

1 tbsp (15 mL) balsamic vinegar

1 cup (250 mL) pear nectar

1/2 tsp (2 mL) sea salt

1/2 tsp (2 mL) black pepper

1 2-lb (900 g) pork tenderloin

1/2 cup (125 mL) crumbled blue cheese

SERVES 4

METHOD

1. In a blender or food processor, combine pears, onion, nectar, balsamic vinegar, basil, thyme, salt and pepper. Using the salsa or pulse button, blend 2 to 3 times.

2. Brush the inside of a large sheet of tin foil with oil. Lay pork tenderloin in center of foil. Spoon pear mixture over tenderloin, sprinkle blue cheese on top and seal foil.

3. Transfer foil-wrapped tenderloin to toaster oven pan and bake at 350°F (175°C) for approximately 25 minutes or until tenderloin is cooked and tender.

This is a dish you'll want to make over and over. The pear, blue cheese and herbs deliciously complement the pork. Serve with garlic mashed potatoes and roasted vegetables on the side.

CHANGE IT UP

VARIATIONS

Substitute pork with beef tenderloin

Substitute gorgonzola or asiago cheese for blue cheese

Substitute apples and apple juice or applesauce for pears and pear nectar and add a hint of cinnamon

Bacon-Wrapped Scallops with Grapefruit, Dill & Vodka

INGREDIENTS

4 slices bacon, cut in half

8 large scallops

8 toothpicks

2 cloves garlic, chopped OR ¹/₂ tsp (2 mL) bottled minced garlic

¹/₂ sweet red pepper, seeded and finely chopped

³/₄ cup (175 mL) freshly squeezed grapefruit juice with pulp

1 oz (28 mL) vodka

¹/₂ cup (125 mL) chopped fresh dill OR 1 tbsp (15 mL) dried

¹/₂ tsp (2 mL) salt

¹/₂ tsp (2 mL) black pepper

You can marinate the bacon-wrapped scallops as little as 4 hours before cooking, but for best results, prepare the evening before and allow the grapefruit, vodka and dill marinade to do its work overnight.

SERVES 2 TO 4

METHOD

1. Wrap a bacon slice around each scallop and secure with a toothpick. Set aside.

2. In a blender or food processor, combine garlic, red pepper, grapefruit juice, vodka, dill, salt and pepper. Set to pulse or chop until well mixed. Reserve one quarter in a small bowl for basting, cover and set aside in the refrigerator.

3. Transfer remaining blender mixture to a large bowl or resealable freezer bag and add scallops. Marinate scallops, covered or sealed, overnight or for at least 4 to 8 hours in the refrigerator.

4. When ready to bake, remove scallops from marinade and place on greased toaster oven pan. Bake at 400°F (205°C), occasionally basting with reserve marinade, for 18 to 20 minutes or until bacon is cooked and scallops are white and opaque.

ENTERTAINING TIP

Use 16 to 20 medium scallops and add Swiss cheese on top in the last 5 minutes of 15 minute cooking time

CHANGE IT UP

VARIATIONS

Substitute 8 jumbo shrimp for scallops

Substitute orange for grapefruit

For a Mexican version, replace grapefruit juice with tomato juice, dill with coriander and vodka with tequila

Swordfish with Dijon & Tarragon

INGREDIENTS

1 sweet red pepper, seeded and finely chopped

3 garlic cloves, chopped OR 1½ tsp (7 mL) bottled minced garlic

1 oz (28 mL) Crème de Menthe liqueur (optional)

1 cup (250 mL) freshly squeezed orange juice OR unsweetened apple juice

¼ cup (50 mL) Dijon mustard

2 tbsp (30 mL) balsamic vinegar

2 tbsp (30 mL) olive oil

½ cup (125 mL) finely chopped fresh tarragon

½ tsp (2 mL) sea salt

½ tsp (2 mL) black pepper

1 large (14 to 16-oz) swordfish steak, cut in two

Perfect for a tête-à-tête, this Dijon-tarragon imbued swordfish is excellent with steamed asparagus and a wild mushroom risotto. Do note that the steaks should be marinating hours (from 4 to 24 hours) before cooking.

SERVES 2

METHOD

1. In a blender or food processor, combine red pepper, garlic, Crème de Menthe (if using), juice, Dijon, balsamic vinegar, oil, tarragon, salt and pepper. Set to pulse and/or chop until mixture is pureed. Reserve half the marinade and set aside.

2. Transfer blender mixture to a large bowl or large resealable freezer bag. Add swordfish, cover or seal, and marinate overnight or for at least 4 to 6 hours in the refrigerator.

3. When ready to cook, remove swordfish steaks from marinade and place in the toaster oven pan. Broil 6 to 8 minutes each side, basting with reserve marinade, until the steaks are done.

ENTERTAINING TIP
Make 1 inch (2.5 cm) squares from swordfish and skewer with cherry tomatoes as hors d'oeuvres

CHANGE IT UP

VARIATIONS
Replace swordfish with other fish such as tuna, sea bass or catfish

Replace tarragon with coriander and add half tsp (2 mL) curry powder

Cajun Burgers with Red Pepper & Parmesan

INGREDIENTS

2 cloves garlic, chopped OR 1 tsp (5 mL) bottled minced garlic

1 small sweet red pepper, seeded and chopped

1 celery stalk, coarsely chopped

1 small red onion, peeled and coarsely chopped

1 jalapeno pepper, seeded and chopped (optional)

1 lb (450 g) lean ground beef

1 egg

1/2 cup (125 mL) grated Parmesan cheese

1/2 cup (125 mL) fine bread crumbs

2 tbsp (30 mL) chili powder

1/2 tsp (2 mL) dried oregano

1/2 tsp (2 mL) sea salt

1/2 tsp (2 mL) black pepper

SERVES 4 TO 6

METHOD

1. In a blender or food processor, combine garlic, red pepper, celery, onion and jalapeno pepper (if using). Set to pulse or chop until vegetables are finely chopped and well combined.

2. Transfer the vegetable mixture to a large bowl and add beef, egg, Parmesan cheese, bread crumbs, chili powder, oregano, salt and pepper. Mix well then shape into 6 to 8 patties.

3. Place two to three patties at a time in a foil-lined toaster oven pan on the broil tray. Broil 3 to 5 minutes each side or until cooked.

The Cajuns, descended from French-speaking settlers who journeyed from Arcadia to the bayous of southern Louisiana, have a distinctive cuisine that incorporates hot peppers. What makes these burgers Cajun is the spicy-hot jalapeno and chili powder.

CHANGE IT UP

VARIATION

Replace Parmesan cheese with half cup (125 mL) grated Swiss or grated cheddar cheese

LOWER FAT OPTION

Use extra-lean ground beef

Use lean ground turkey

Use light or low-fat Parmesan cheese

SPICY

Add half tsp (2 mL) cayenne pepper to step 1

Curry Lamb Chops with Mint

INGREDIENTS

1 small onion, coarsely chopped

2 cloves garlic, chopped OR 1 tsp (5 mL) bottled minced garlic

1/2 cup (125 mL) plain yogurt

1/2 cup (125 mL) chopped fresh mint OR 1 tbsp (15 mL) dried

1/4 cup (50 mL) orange juice

2 tbsp (30 mL) olive oil

2 tbsp (30 mL) mild curry powder

1 oz (28 mL) Ouzo liqueur (optional)

1/2 tsp (2 mL) sea salt

1/2 tsp (2 mL) black pepper

6 lamb chops, each 3/4 inch thick

SERVES 2 TO 4

METHOD

1. In a blender or food processor, combine onion, garlic, yogurt, mint, orange juice, oil, curry powder, Ouzo (if using), salt and pepper. Set to pulse/purée and/or chop until puréed. Reserve half and set aside.

2. Transfer blender mixture into a large bowl. Add lamb, cover and marinate for 4 to 8 hours, or overnight in the refrigerator.

3. When ready to cook, place two to three chops at a time in the toaster pan on the broil tray. Broil 8 to 10 minutes each side, basting with reserved marinade.

4. Spoon remaining marinade on top and serve.

The curry-orange-mint-yogurt mixture, used to marinate the lamb, also makes for a great sauce or accompaniment to other spicy meats. If possible, use fresh mint, rather than dried; fresh herbs really do make a difference. And do note that this recipe requires advance preparation: the lamb should be marinating for hours (anywhere from 4 to 24 hours) before cooking.

CHANGE IT UP

VARIATION

Substitute 6 large portobello mushrooms for lamb, but skip the marinating step and use marinade as a sauce

Substitute beef steak or chicken for lamb

LOWER FAT OPTION

Use non-fat plain yogurt

SPICY

Substitute the mild curry powder for hot curry powder

Almond Biscotti with Cinnamon & Maple Syrup

INGREDIENTS

1/2 cup (125 mL) unsalted butter, softened

1/2 cup (125 mL) granulated sugar

1 large egg

1 tsp (5 mL) vanilla extract

1/4 cup (50 mL) maple syrup

2 cups (500 mL) all-purpose flour

1 tsp (5 mL) baking powder

A pinch of salt

1 tsp (5 mL) ground cinnamon

1/2 cup (125 mL) slivered almonds

The secret to making perfect biscotti is usually in the wrist – in this recipe, the secret is in the maple syrup, a flavour supplement that tastes divine, especially when the biscotti is liberally dipped in espresso or maple tea. (Once made, these can be stored for up to one month in an airtight container.)

MAKES 20 TO 30 small biscotti

METHOD

1. In a food processor, combine butter and sugar. Blend until light and fluffy. Add egg and mix well. Continue blending and add vanilla and maple syrup. Add the flour, baking powder, salt, cinnamon and almonds and mix well.

2. Meanwhile, line toaster oven pan with parchment paper. Remove biscotti batter and, using your hands, roll dough into 2 logs, the length of the pan and roughly 2 inches in diameter.

3. Place biscotti logs on parchment-lined pan and transfer to toaster oven. Bake on top level at 350°F (205°C) for 25 minutes or until golden brown. Remove and let cool for 10 minutes.

4. Place logs on cutting board and, using a serrated knife, slice each log diagonally at a 45-degree angle into half inch (1 cm) pieces. Lay flat on baking pan and return to toaster oven. Bake for 5 minutes, turn over, and bake for another 5 minutes more or until slightly dried and golden brown all over.

CHANGE IT UP

VARIATION

Substitute half cup (125 mL) raisins, walnuts or cashews for the almonds

Sesame Honey Garlic Chicken with Salsa

INGREDIENTS

1/2 cup (125 mL) liquid honey

1/2 cup (125 mL) salsa

1/4 cup (50 mL) sesame oil

1/4 cup (50 mL) olive oil

4 large garlic cloves, finely chopped OR 2 tsp (10 mL) bottled minced garlic

1 tbsp (15 mL) chili powder

1/2 tsp (2 mL) paprika

1/2 tsp (2 mL) sea salt

1 tsp (5 mL) black pepper

2 boneless, skinless chicken breasts

SERVES 2

METHOD

1. In a blender or food processor, combine honey, salsa, sesame oil, olive oil, garlic, chili powder, paprika, salt and pepper. Set to pulse and blend until dressing emulsifies. Reserve half and set aside, covered, in the refrigerator.

2. In a medium bowl or large resealable freezer bag, add chicken. Transfer dressing in blender to bowl or bag and toss well. Marinate chicken overnight or for at least 4 to 6 hours, covered, in the refrigerator.

3. When ready to cook, transfer chicken to foil-lined toaster oven pan and bake at 350°F (175°C) for approximately 25 minutes, basting twice with reserved marinade.

Although it can be done 4 to 6 hours in advance, it's best to marinate the chicken overnight in the honey-sesame-salsa oil dressing. Serve this with roasted sweet potatoes and/or a minted pea and pearl onion salad.

CHANGE IT UP

VARIATIONS

Substitute 1 1/2 to 2 lb pork tenderloin for chicken

Replace the toaster oven with the electric grill and grill 12 minutes on each side

LOWER FAT OPTION

Replace sesame oil with orange juice and use half the amount of honey

Orange Garlic Basil Shrimp

INGREDIENTS

1/2 cup (125 mL) olive oil

3 cloves garlic, chopped OR 1 tsp (5 mL) bottled minced garlic

1/2 cup (125 mL) freshly squeezed orange juice with pulp

1/2 sweet red pepper, seeded and finely chopped

1 tbsp (15 mL) freshly squeezed lemon juice

2 tbsp (30 mL) balsamic vinegar OR 1 tbsp (15 mL) granulated sugar

1 tsp (5 mL) dried basil

1 lb (450 g) large shrimp, shelled and deveined

1 tbsp (15 mL) grated orange zest

The orange-garlic-basil sauce makes these shrimp more succulent than most. Serve skewered on a pilaf, or mixed in with pasta.

SERVES 4

METHOD

1. In a blender or food processor, combine oil, garlic, orange juice, pepper, lemon juice, balsamic vinegar and basil. Set to pulse and/or chop until well mixed.

2. Transfer blender mixture to a large bowl or resealable freezer bag and add shrimp. Marinate the shrimp, covered or sealed, overnight or for at least 6 to 8 hours, in the refrigerator.

3. When ready to bake, remove shrimp from marinade and place on greased toaster oven pan. Bake at 450°F (230°C) for approximately 5 minutes. Add the orange zest and broil for 2 minutes more.

VEGETARIAN OPTION
Replace shrimp with a combination of vegetables such as onions, celery, fennel, carrots, egg plant or zucchini, chopped into large pieces.

ENTERTAINING TIP
For hors d'oeuvres: substitute smaller shrimp for large and, when cooked, serve on toasted, thinly sliced French bread spread with goat cheese.

CHANGE IT UP

VARIATIONS

Substitute 1 lb (450 g) medium scallops for shrimp

Replace dried basil with half cup (125 mL) fresh and add to food processor in first step

SPICY

To give these shrimp a bit of heat, add 1 tsp (5 mL) hot sauce to the marinade

Roasted Vegetables with Dijon, Rosemary & Balsamic

INGREDIENTS

1/2 cup (125 mL) olive oil

3 cloves garlic, chopped OR 1 tsp (5 mL) bottled minced garlic

2 tbsp (30 mL) Dijon mustard

1/4 cup (50 mL) white wine

1/4 cup (50 mL) balsamic vinegar

1 tsp (5 mL) dried rosemary OR 2 tbsp (30 mL) fresh

1/2 tsp (2 mL) sea salt

1 tsp (5 mL) black pepper

1 small red onion, peeled and quartered

1 cup (250 mL) peeled baby carrots

2 celery stalks, each cut in half

1 cup (250 mL) green beans

1 sweet red pepper, seeded and cut into large pieces

1 green pepper, seeded and cut into large pieces

6 asparagus spears, ends trimmed

These are my favourite roasted vegetables: I serve this dish for Thanksgiving dinners, and in spring, usually with roasted chicken or turkey.

SERVES 4

METHOD

1. In a blender or food processor, combine olive oil, garlic, Dijon mustard, wine, balsamic vinegar, rosemary, salt and pepper. Set to pulse and blend until dressing is emulsified. Reserve 1/4 cup (50 mL) and set aside.

2. In a large bowl or large resealable freezer bag, combine onion, carrots, celery, beans, peppers and asparagus. Transfer dressing in blender to bowl or bag and toss vegetables. Marinate for 2 to 4 hours, covered or sealed, in the refrigerator.

3. When fully marinated, transfer vegetables to toaster oven foil-lined pan and bake at 350°F (205°C) for 40 minutes.

4. Transfer roasted vegetables to a large bowl, toss with reserved dressing, and serve.

ENTERTAINING TIP

In a food processor, purée half the roasted vegetables with 1 cup (250 mL) sour cream to make a vegetable dip. Serve on garlic toast.

CHANGE IT UP

ADDITION

Add 8 large shrimp and, in a large skillet with oil, stir fry with vegetables for 12 to 15 minutes or until shrimp are pink

SPICY

For hot and spicy vegetables, add 1 tsp (5 mL) hot sauce to step 1

Ken's Orange Biscuits

INGREDIENTS

3 cups (750 mL) all-purpose flour

1 cup (250 mL) quick-cooking rolled oats

1/2 cup (125 mL) granulated sugar

3 tbsp (45 mL) baking powder

1 tsp (5 mL) ground nutmeg

1 tsp (5 mL) ground cinnamon

1/2 tsp (2 mL) salt

1 large egg

1/2 cup (125 mL) whole milk

1/2 cup (125 mL) sour cream

3 tbsp (45 mL) grated orange zest

1 cup (250 mL) freshly squeezed orange juice

The word "biscuit" comes from the French word roughly meaning "twice cooked". However, whenever the word "Ken's" appears with it, you'll know it translates into "very easy". In this instance, just throw everything into the processor, roll, flatten and then bake in the toaster oven. The result is a delicious, citrus-y biscuit, perfect for tea.

MAKES 15 TO 20 cookies

METHOD

1. In a food processor, combine flour, oats, sugar, baking powder, nutmeg, cinnamon and salt. Set to pulse and mix well. Add the egg, milk, sour cream, zest and orange juice and continue processing until thoroughly mixed.

2. Meanwhile, spray toaster oven pan with vegetable oil. Remove batter from food processor, one tablespoon at a time, and roll into a ball. Place on the pan – leaving enough space between each ball, about 2 inches – and flatten with your finger. Continue doing this until tray is full. Repeat until all dough has been baked.

3. Transfer pan to toaster oven and bake at 375°F (190 °C) for about 25 minutes or until golden brown.

CHANGE IT UP

LOWER FAT OPTION

Substitute skim milk for whole milk

Substitute non-fat sour cream for sour cream

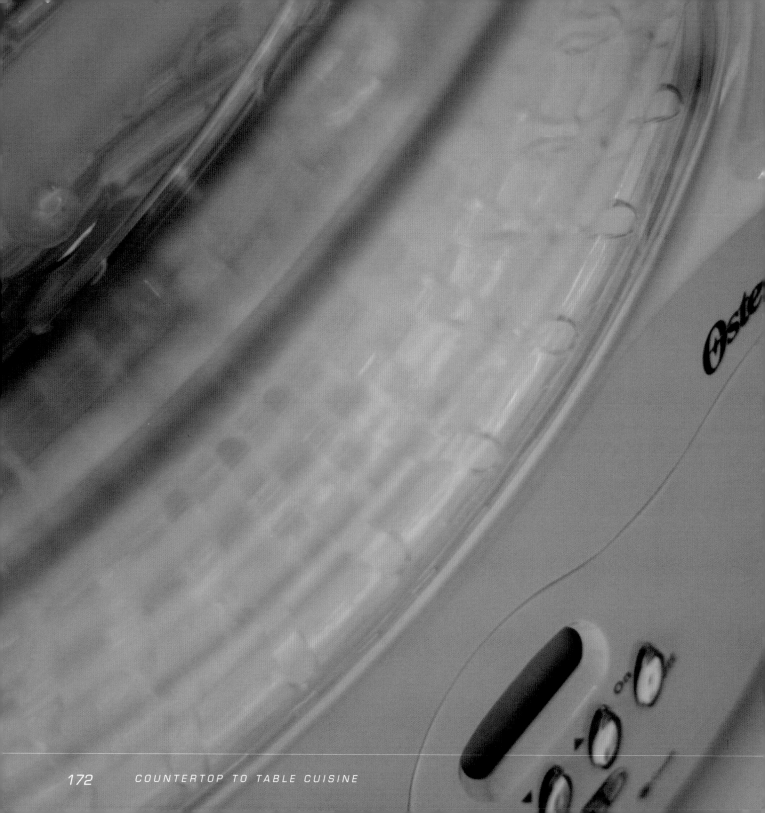

COUNTERTOP TO TABLE CUISINE

DIGITAL
FOOD STEAMER

Steam Power!

Many people think steamers are only for rice and vegetables. No! It's true that steamed vegetables do taste crisper, fresher and retain more of their vitamins and nutrients. But you can steam almost any food, and with the right spices and ingredients they will not only be a delicious meal, but a wholesome and healthy one, as well. Steaming is a great way to reduce fat and oils in your diet and with these recipes and the easy-to-use Oster® Digital Food Steamer the results are perfect every time. Vitamins, nutrients, great taste without added fats or oils – that's what will get you steaming toward a healthy lifestyle.

Fennel Swordfish with Tarragon & Crème de Menthe
Garlic Chicken with White Wine & Red Onion
Steamed Citrus Shrimp & Scallops with Basil
Spicy Sirloin with Portobello Mushrooms & Red Wine
Cornucopia of Mushrooms with Onions & Green Peppers
Salmon Steaks with Chunky Grapefruit Sauce
Steamed Vegetables with Apples & Blue Cheese

Fennel Swordfish with Tarragon & Crème de Menthe

INGREDIENTS

1 fennel bulb, coarsely chopped

1 small red onion, coarsely chopped

1 medium carrot, peeled, coarsely chopped

1/2 cup (125 mL) unsweetened apple juice

2 oz (86 mL) Crème de Menthe liqueur

1/2 cup (125 mL) chopped fresh tarragon

1 tsp (5 mL) granulated sugar

1/2 tsp (2 mL) sea salt

1/2 tsp (2 mL) black pepper

2 10-oz swordfish steaks

SERVES 2 TO 4

METHOD

1. In a blender or food processor, combine fennel, onion, carrot, apple juice, Crème de Menthe, tarragon, sugar, salt and pepper. Set to pulse and/or chop until vegetables are finely chopped and well mixed.

2. Place the swordfish into an electric steamer, cutting each steak in half to fit.

3. Transfer fennel mixture on top of swordfish and steam 12 to 15 minutes or until swordfish is white and flaky.

GRILLING OPTIONAL
Instead of steaming, grill swordfish for 7 to 8 minutes each side, and serve chunky sauce on the side.

TOASTER OVEN OPTION
Instead of steaming, broil swordfish in toaster oven, broiling for 15 minutes or until swordfish is opaque.

This swordfish is especially delicious imbued with licorice, mint and tarragon flavours. Serve this with a carrot-raisin cole slaw or a carrot and parsnip soup with dill cream.

CHANGE IT UP

VARIATION
Substitute swordfish with 2 tuna steaks or 4 skinless, boneless chicken breasts

Garlic Chicken with White Wine & Red Onion

INGREDIENTS

1 cup (250 mL) white wine

1/4 cup (50 mL) olive oil

1/2 cup (125 mL) plain yogurt OR sour cream

6 cloves garlic, chopped

1 tsp (5 mL) chili powder

1/2 tsp (2 mL) dried basil

1/2 tsp (2 mL) dried thyme

1/2 tsp (2 mL) sea salt

1/2 tsp (2 mL) black pepper

2 boneless, skinless chicken breasts

3 red onions, thickly sliced

SERVES 2

METHOD

1. In a blender or food processor, combine wine, oil, yogurt, garlic, chili powder, basil, thyme, salt and pepper. Mix well.

2. Transfer half the mixture to a medium bowl or large resealable freezer bag, add chicken, cover or seal and marinate for 4 to 6 hours or overnight in the refrigerator.

3. When ready, discard marinade and place chicken in an electric steamer. Arrange onions on top of chicken and steam for 15 minutes. Using half the reserved marinade, drizzle over onions and chicken.

4. Steam for another 6 to 10 minutes or until chicken is thoroughly cooked. Drizzle remaining marinade over chicken and onions and serve.

This recipe requires advance preparation: be sure to prepare wine marinade a day before and marinate chicken overnight in the refrigerator. Your chicken will be especially succulent. Serve with shoestring sweet potato fries (baked, to make it healthier) and an avocado, tomato, onion salad.

CHANGE IT UP

VARIATION

Substitute chicken with 6 to 8 oz turkey, pork, fish or seafood

LOWER FAT OPTION

Substitute non-fat plain yogurt or non-fat sour cream for the yogurt and sour cream, and omit olive oil

SPICY

Add half tsp (2 mL) cayenne pepper when combining ingredients in step 1

Steamed Citrus Shrimp & Scallops with Basil

INGREDIENTS

1 small red onion, coarsely chopped

4 garlic cloves, coarsely chopped

1/4 cup chopped fresh basil OR 1 tbsp (15 mL) dried

2 cups (500 mL) orange juice

2 tbsp (30 mL) lemon juice

2 tbsp (30 mL) liquid honey

2 tbsp (30 mL) olive oil

2 tbsp (30 mL) soy sauce

1/2 tsp (2 mL) black pepper

12 large scallops

24 large shrimp, peeled and cleaned

SERVES 4

METHOD

1. In a blender or food processor, combine onion, garlic, basil, lemon and orange juice, honey, oil, soy sauce and pepper. Set to pulse and/or chop and blend until smooth.

2. Reserve 1/2 cup (125 mL) and set aside, covered, in refrigerator.

3. Transfer remaining mixture into a bowl or large resealable freezer bag. Add the seafood and marinate, covered or sealed, in the refrigerator overnight or for at least 4 to 6 hours prior to steaming.

4. When seafood is fully marinated, transfer to an electric steamer and set for 15 minutes. Half way through the steaming process, carefully remove lid and drizzle with the reserved mixture.

I usually serve citrus and basil-flavoured steamed shrimp and scallops on a bed of greens, but these also taste great tossed into a bowl of lightly oiled or buttered linguine. Do note that the seafood needs to be marinated hours – even overnight – before serving.

CHANGE IT UP

VARIATION

Substitute lobster, salmon, tuna or swordfish for shrimp and scallops

Spicy Sirloin with Portobello Mushrooms & Red Wine

INGREDIENTS

1 large sirloin steak, cut in half

4 large portobello mushrooms

MARINADE

2 cups (500 mL) red wine

1 small onion, minced

2 cloves garlic, minced OR 1 tsp (5 mL) bottled minced garlic

1/4 cup (50 mL) olive oil

2 tbsp (30 mL) balsamic vinegar

1/2 tsp (2 mL) sea salt

1/2 tsp (2 mL) black pepper

DRY MIXTURE

1 tbsp (15 mL) chili powder

1 tsp (5 mL) dried basil

1 tsp (5 mL) dried rosemary

1 tsp (5 mL) garlic powder

1 tsp (5 mL) onion powder

1/2 tsp (2 mL) cayenne pepper

1/2 tsp (2 mL) sea salt

1/2 tsp (2 mL) black pepper

SERVES 2 TO 4

METHOD

1. In a large bowl or a large resealable freezer bag, combine red wine, onion, garlic, oil, balsamic vinegar, salt and pepper. Mix well. Add steak and marinate, covered in the refrigerator, overnight or for at least 6 to 8 hours prior to steaming.

2. Meanwhile, in a small bowl, combine chili powder, basil, rosemary, garlic powder, onion powder, cayenne, salt and pepper. Mix well and set aside.

3. When marinated steaks are ready for steaming, remove from marinade and, along with mushrooms, dredge in the dry mixture, lightly coating all sides. Place steaks and mushrooms in an electric steamer and set to 18 minutes for a medium-done steak. Adjust timing to doneness of the steak.

Sirloin steak and portobello mushrooms have got to be one of the most mouthwatering combinations. Use the dry mixture – or rub – in this recipe on any other meats, fish or vegetable you steam or grill.

CHANGE IT UP

VARIATION

Substitute 2 8-oz skinless, boneless chicken breasts for sirloin steak

Cornucopia of Mushrooms with Onions & Green Peppers

INGREDIENTS

1 tsp (5 mL) dried basil

1 tsp (5 mL) dried rosemary

1 tsp (5 mL) dried thyme

1 tsp (5 mL) chili powder

1 tbsp (15 mL) garlic powder

1/2 tsp (2 mL) sea salt

1 tsp (5 mL) black pepper

3 medium portobello mushrooms, thickly sliced

2 cups (500 mL) button mushrooms, cut in half

1 cup (250 mL) cremini mushrooms, cut in half

1 cup (250 mL) shiitake mushrooms, cut in half

2 green peppers, sliced

1 large red onion, sliced

SERVES 4 TO 6

METHOD

1. In a small bowl, combine basil, rosemary, thyme, chili powder, garlic powder, salt and pepper. Mix well and set aside.

2. In a large bowl, combine mushrooms, peppers and onions. Mix well. Sprinkle the dry mixture, saving 1/4 as reserve.

3. Place the mushrooms and vegetables into an electric steamer and set for 12 minutes. Carefully remove lid, add reserved dry mixture and steam another 5 minutes before serving.

GRILLING OPTION
Instead of steaming, cook mushrooms on an indoor grill

If you love mushrooms, you'll adore this recipe, which calls for cremini, shiitake and portobello mushrooms, along with the ubiquitous but humble, button. Of course, if you can't find, shiitake or cremini, you can always substitute with another variety.

CHANGE IT UP

SPICY
Add 1 tsp (5 mL) cayenne pepper to dry mixture in step 1

Salmon Steaks with Chunky Grapefruit Sauce

INGREDIENTS

1/2 cup (125 mL) grapefruit juice

2 8-oz salmon steaks

1/2 cup (125 mL) coarsely chopped grapefruit

1/2 cup (125 mL) grapefruit juice with pulp

1/4 cup (60 mL) liquid honey

2 tbsp (30 mL) balsamic vinegar

1 small red onion, coarsely chopped

1/2 tsp (2 mL) sea salt

1/2 tsp (2 mL) white pepper

SERVES 2 TO 4

METHOD

1. In a medium bowl or large resealable freezer bag, combine grapefruit juice and salmon. Marinate, covered or sealed in the refrigerator, for 4 to 6 hours, or overnight.

2. Meanwhile, in a food processor, combine chopped grapefruit and juice with pulp, honey, balsamic vinegar, onion, salt and pepper. Process until sauce is chunky.

3. When salmon is ready, remove from marinade and transfer to an electric steamer. Add sauce and steam for 15 to 18 minutes or until salmon is pink.

4. Top salmon with sauce and serve.

The tartness of this recipe is tempered by the honey and balsamic vinegar. For a complete meal, serve with a black-bean salsa on the side.

CHANGE IT UP

VARIATIONS

Substitute 2 tuna steaks or 2 chicken breasts for salmon

Substitute equivalent amounts of orange for grapefruit

SPICY

Add 1 tsp (5 mL) hot sauce to step 2

Steamed Vegetables with Apples & Blue Cheese

INGREDIENTS

1 tsp (5 mL) dried basil

1 tsp (5 mL) dried thyme

1 tsp (5 mL) dried rosemary

1/2 tsp (2 mL) cinnamon

1/2 tsp (2 mL) sea salt

1/2 tsp (2 mL) black pepper

2 sweet red peppers, seeded and cut into thin strips

2 green peppers, seeded and cut into thin strips

1 large onion, thinly sliced

2 carrots, sliced thinly on the diagonal

8 asparagus spears, ends cut

1 cup (250 mL) chopped green beans, cut once on diagonal

1 cup (250 mL) cauliflower florets

2 apples, peeled, cored and sliced

1/2 cup (125 mL) crumbled blue cheese

SERVES 4 TO 6

METHOD

1. In a small bowl, combine basil, thyme, rosemary, cinnamon, salt and pepper. Mix well.

2. In another bowl, combine peppers, onion, carrots, asparagus, green beans, cauliflower and apples. Sprinkle dry mixture liberally over vegetables.

3. Set an electric steamer to 15 minutes; add vegetables and cover.

4. Two minutes prior to completion, carefully remove steamer lid and sprinkle blue cheese on top. Return cover and allow to steam until done. Mix and serve while still warm.

The blue cheese, mixed in at the end of the steaming process, gives this crisp vegetable-apple medley a real bite. Serve with soup and pasta on a chilly fall evening.

CHANGE IT UP

VARIATIONS

Substitute half cup (125 mL) crumbled goat cheese or feta for blue cheese

Substitute 2 pears, peeled, cored and sliced, for apples

Cooking Terms Glossary

Cooking has its own vocabulary just as any other activity. Although not all-inclusive, this glossary is a handy reference for both beginning and experience cooks. We've included examples of foods, in most cases, to help you quickly familiarize yourself with the terms.

Bakes: Cook in oven surrounded by dry heat. Bake uncovered for dry, crisp surfaces (breads, cakes, cookies, chicken) or covered for moistness (vegetables, casseroles, stews).

Baste: Spoon liquid over food (pan juices over turkey) during cooking to keep it moist.

Batter: An uncooked mixture of flour, eggs and liquid with other ingredients; thin enough to be spooned or poured (muffins, pancakes).

Blanch: Plunge food into boiling water for a brief time to preserve colour, texture and nutritional value or to remove skin (vegetables, fruits, nuts).

Boil: Heat liquid until bubbles rise continuously and break on the surface and steam is given off. For rolling boil, the bubbles form rapidly.

Caramelize: Melt sugar slowly over low heat until it becomes a golden brown, caramel-flavoured syrup. Or sprinkle granulated, powdered or brown sugar on top of a food, then place under a broiler until the sugar is melted and caramelized.

Chop: Cut into coarse or fine irregular pieces, using knife, food chopper, blender or food processor.

Coat: Cover food evenly with crumbs or sauce.

Cool: Allow hot food to stand at room temperature for a specified amount of time. Placing hot food on a wire rack will help it cool more quickly. Stirring mixtures occasionally also will help them cool more quickly and evenly.

Core: Remove the centre of a fruit (apple, pear, pineapple). Cores contain small seeds (apple, pear) or are woody in texture (pineapple).

Crisp-tender: Doneness description of vegetables cooked until they retain some of the crisp texture of the raw food.

Crush: Press into very fine particles (crushing a clove of garlic, using chef's knife or garlic press).

Cube: Cut food into squares 1/2 inch or larger, using knife.

Cut up: Cut into small irregular pieces with kitchen scissors or knife. Or cut into smaller pieces (broiler-fryer chicken).

Dash: Less than 1/8 teaspoon or an ingredient.

Deep-fry or French-fry: Cook in hot fat that's deep enough to float the food.

Dice: Cut food into square smaller than 1/2 inch, using knife.

Dot: Drop small pieces of an ingredient (margarine or butter) randomly over food (sliced apples in an apple pie).

Dough: Mixture of flour and liquid with other ingredients (often including a leavening); it is stiff but pliable. Dough can be dropped from a spoon (cookies), rolled (pie crust) or kneaded (bread).

Drain: Pour off liquid by putting the food into a strainer or colander that has been set in the sink. If draining fat from meat, place strainer in disposable container. If liquid is to be saved, place the strainer in a bowl or other container.

Dredge: To coat food evenly with dry ingredients such as flour.

Drizzle: Pour topping in thin lines from a spoon or liquid measuring cup in an uneven pattern over food (glaze on a cake, cookies).

Dust: Sprinkle lightly with flour, cornmeal, powdered sugar or cocoa; for example, dust coffee cake with powdered sugar.

Emulsify: To completely blend together an oil with an acid such as vinegar or lemon.

Flake: Break lightly into small pieces, using fork; for example, flaking cooked fish.

Flute: Squeeze pastry edge with fingers to make a finished, ornamental edge.

Fry: Cook in hot fat over moderate or high heat. Also see Panfry and Sauté.

Glaze: Brush, spread or drizzle an ingredient or mixture of ingredients (jam, melted chocolate) on hot or cold foods to give a glossy appearance or hard finish.

Grate: Rub a hard-textured food against the small, rough, sharp-edged holes of a grater, reducing them to tiny particles (citrus peel, chocolate, Parmesan cheese). For citrus peel, grate only the skin, not the bitter white membrane.

Grease: Rub the inside surface of a pan with shortening, using pastry brush, waxed paper or paper towel, to prevent food from sticking during baking (muffins, some casseroles). Nonstick cooking spray may also be used. Margarine and butter usually contain salt that may cause hot foods to stick.

Grease and Flour: Rub the inside surface of a pan with shortening before dusting it with flour, to prevent food from sticking during baking, such as cakes. After flouring the pan, turn the pan upside down, and tap the bottom to remove excess flour.

Heat Oven: Turn the oven controls to the desired temperature, allowing the oven to heat thoroughly before adding food. Heating takes about 10 minutes for most ovens. Also called preheating.

Julienne: Cut into thin, match like strips, using knife or food processor; for example, fruits, vegetables, meats.

Knead: Work dough on a floured surface into a smooth, elastic mass, using hands or an electric mixer with dough hooks. Kneading develops the gluten in flour and results in an even texture and a smooth, rounded top. It can take up to about 15 minutes by hand.

Marinate: Let food stand in a savoury, usually acidic liquid in a glass or plastic container for several hours to add flavour or to tenderize. Marinade is the savoury liquid in which the food is marinated.

Mince: Cut food into very fine pieces, smaller than chopped food.

Panfry: Fry meat or other food, starting with a cold skillet, using little or no fat and usually pouring off fat from meat as it accumulates during cooking.

Peel: Cut off outer covering, using knife or vegetable peeler (apples, potatoes). Also, to strip off outer covering, using fingers (bananas, oranges).

Poach: Cook in simmering liquid just below the boiling point (eggs, fish).

Purée: Vegetables, fruits, etc., blended to produce a smooth, finely divided texture.

Reduce: Boil liquid uncovered to evaporate liquid and intensify the flavour.

Roast: Cook meat uncovered on rack in shallow pan in oven without adding liquid.

Sauté: Cook over medium-high heat in hot fat with frequent tossing or turning motion.

Scald: Heat liquid to just below the boiling point. Tiny bubbles will form at the edge. A thin skin will form on the top of milk.

Score: Cut surface of food about 1/4 inch deep, using knife, to facilitate cooking, flavouring, tenderizing or for appearance (meat, yeast bread).

Shred: Cut into long, thin pieces, using round, smooth holes of shredder, a knife or food processor (cabbage, carrots, cheese).

Simmer: Cook in liquid on range top, just below the boiling point. Usually done after reducing heat from a boil. Bubbles will rise slowly and break just below the surface.

Slice: Cut into uniform-size flat pieces (bread, meat).

Soft Peaks: Egg whites beaten until peaks are rounded or curl when beaters are lifted from bowl, while still moist and glossy. Also see Stiff Peaks.

Soften: Let cold food stand at room temperature, or microwave at low power setting, until no longer hard (margarine, butter, cream cheese).

Steam: Cook food by placing on a rack or special steamer basket over a small amount of boiling or simmering water in a covered pan. Steaming helps retain flavour, shape, colour, texture and nutritional value.

Stew: Cook slowly in a small amount of liquid for a long time (stewed fruit, beef stew).

Stiff Peaks: Egg whites beaten until peaks stand up straight when beaters are lifted from bowl, while still moist and glossy. Also see Soft Peaks.

Stir-fry: A Chinese method of cooking uniform pieces of food in small amount of hot oil over high heat, stirring constantly.

Strain: Pour mixture or liquid through a fine sieve or strainer to remove larger particles.

Tear: Break into pieces, using fingers (lettuce for salads; bread slices for soft bread crumbs).

Toss: Tumble ingredients lightly with a lifting motion, such as a salad with greens.

Zest: A grated piece of the rind of an orange or lemon.

Ken's Oster® Appliances Review

Oster® Digital Food Steamer

I had a lot of fun using the steamer. You can actually do a whole meal in the steamer in 20 to 25 minutes! This book is all about health and diet and this unit brings both to your table. I even did steak in the steamer with vegetables. Cooking with steam really is an interesting concept; you retain the important nutrients of the food and don't have to give in on the flavour. I like an appliance that lets you press a button and walk away while it does its job.

Oster® Inspire® 6-Slice Toaster Oven

Yes, a toaster oven. My feeling now is how can you live without a toaster oven. I use my toaster oven every single day and not just to make toast or warm things up. I use the toaster oven for broiling to baking to making a whole breakfast with a flick of a button. I love the fact a toaster oven uses less energy and does not heat up the kitchen.

Oster® Inspire® Rice Cooker

Yes, it does rice to perfection. And if you hate cooking on a conventional stovetop and having that rice pot soaking for a week because everything stuck to the bottom, this appliance is for you. No problem like that with this rice cooker and it will keep anything you create nice and warm. I make pasta, soups, stews and several different rice dishes, even risotto. The rice cooker has enough volume to feed a whole family or is perfect just for two. Again, an appliance that you can press a button and let it work its magic.

Oster® Commercial Style Deep Fryer

I have never had a home deep fryer and now will not live without this amazing appliance. I use the deep fryer to make the most incredible french fries, onion rings, fish or even vegetables. Fried foods should be eaten in moderation, so I combine my fried foods with other dishes prepared in the skillet, steamer, indoor grill or toaster oven. For example, steamed fish with very thin french fries or grilled chicken and onion rings.

Oster® Inspire® Indoor Grill

Wow, being able to grill your food inside year 'round is not crazy but a reality with this smokeless grill. Nothing is better than the wonderful flavour of grilled food whether it is seafood, poultry, vegetables or your favourite meat. The indoor grill is an appliance that encourages you to try grilling more than just meat. Clean up is a snap and again you are using very little energy.

Oster® Inspire® Electric Skillet

I absolutely love this skillet. The reason – its versatility. It does everything, sautéing, poaching, rice dishes and even some pasta dishes, all in one pot. The skillet is not limited to just bacon and eggs or pancakes, which it does fabulously, but I also use it as a wok to stir-fry, poach chicken and fish and have done incredible rice and pasta dishes. The skillet is perfect for low fat cooking, with the non-stick surface you don't have to add additional oil or butter. The surface makes clean up so easy and the updated design makes it "IN" to have on your countertop.

Oster® Blender

Guess what? The blender is not just an appliance to mix drinks. Yes, it does that well, but simplify your life and use the blender to chop vegetables or combine ingredients and recipes in one step. I use this appliance to prepare a "Soup in a Blender" or even a "Breakfast in a Blender". I would have to say that my blender is one of the most used appliances in Ken's Kitchen. Save more time preparing your meals and spend more time with your family and friends.

Oster® Programmable Coffeemaker

What can you do with this appliance besides making really good coffee every day? Use the coffee in your recipes. The flavour of coffee is an ingredient that takes average food to a different level. I use coffee in different recipes from grilling to baking to one-pot meals like chili. Try the array of flavoured coffees and espresso in every day food. It adds that robust nutty flavour that will have your company wondering what that secret ingredient is in your recipe. Instead of alcohol in a recipe replace it with coffee and you'll be a hit when entertaining.

Oster® Inspire® Food Processor

Like the skillet, this food processor is very versatile and can save you an enormous amount of time in preparing ingredients. I like to use it for chopping and mixing ingredients not only for traditional recipes but also for marinades, salad dressings or dry ingredients for coatings. For anything you want chopped, mixed or well blended, this is an indispensable appliance. The volume this appliance can handle is another plus, as being able to do a task in one step is very important for quick meals.

Acknowledgements

I would like to take this opportunity to thank the many people and organizations who made this book possible.

Adam Ball, Sunbeam Corporation (Canada) Ltd.
Urban advertising + design
Joe and Wanda Urban
Trevor Shaw
Don Davies
Jean Katchanoski
Kyle Wehrle
Mike and Poppy Zozula
James Scott, Food Stylist/Props
David Acacia, Food Stylist/Prep
Gill Humphreys
Todd Ross
Kirk MacKenzie
Nicole de Montbrun
Larry Feldman
Bob Burnett
Lorie Crawford
Andy and Thia
Paul and Helen
Manny and Rosa
David Church
Staff – Marina Quay West, Toronto
Derlea Foods
Cilento Wines

Napoleon my nasty Chihuahua and Gypsy my wondering cat.

INDEX